LITTLE WHITE LIES

and the

SEVEN DEADLY SINS

A Faith-Fun Look at Daily Life

LAUREL JACKSON

WESTBOW
P R E S S®
A DIVISION OF THOMAS NELSON
& ZONDERVAN

WestBow Press books may be ordered through booksellers or by contacting:

WestBow Press
A Division of Thomas Nelson & Zondervan
1663 Liberty Drive
Bloomington, IN 47403
www.westbowpress.com
1 (866) 928-1240

ISBN: 978-1-9736-2782-1 (sc)
ISBN: 978-1-9736-2784-5 (hc)
ISBN: 978-1-9736-2783-8 (e)

Library of Congress Control Number: 2018905496

Print information available on the last page.

WestBow Press rev. date: 05/30/2018

CONTENTS

PROLOGUE

HOW THIS BOOK CAME ABOUT

I grew up in the church. Now, I don't mean in the Old Testament Samuel *my-mom-dropped-me-off-to-be-raised-by-the-priest* sort of way, but in the *if-you-skip-one-Sunday-of-church-the-heavens-will-come-crashing-down-on-you* sort of way. In fact, on the one Sunday I did actually skip church because I told my parents I was "sick" (wink-wink), I recall resting my weary twelve-year-old body comfortably on the couch, where I started to think of all the wonderful things I could do for the next couple of hours while my parents and three brothers were away. Just about that time, I looked out the window and noticed a dark cloud heading toward our Central Washington town. Within a few minutes, the dark cloud had completely engulfed the sky around our valley. My parents returned home about a half-hour after they had left, because church was cancelled. It turned out that I managed to play hooky from worship on the day that Mt. St. Helens erupted: May 18, 1980. I figured that my lying to my parents and claiming that I was sick when, in fact, I wasn't, had actually caused the mountain to blow. There was no way I was going to take that chance again, so I've been attending church faithfully ever since.

But faithful attendance at the local house of worship doesn't always equal faithful attention—at least, that's how it's been for me, and more often than I really care to admit. And, it's often been my fault. Sometimes my distraction during a church service—then and now—has stemmed from planning for the future, or stressing over a test, or dreaming about a boy, or coming up with next week's menu (those little pew envelopes are just the right size for shopping lists, aren't they?), or something else that's equally important.

Other times, however, the service has been downright boring. And to be sure that it's not just me, I've often looked around at those people in the pews near me to see if they felt similarly. One time, I caught my younger brother dead asleep at the end of the pew. His head was down. Way down. He was leaning on the arm rest, and my dad, who was sitting next to him, gave an elbow to the kidney to wake him up. Steve didn't even flinch. He responded with, "I'm praying," and continued his nap.

Idle hands may be the devil's tools, but I contend that idle minds— bored ones in particular—aren't much better. While in high school, as I sat in the church pew one particularly uninteresting (and hot and sticky) summer Sunday morning, I thought, *How great would it be to have a worship service that people actually liked coming to?*

Would it really be all that difficult? So that's what I aspired to: creating a worship service that was interesting. And enjoyable. One that you were excited to be part of; one that you were a little sad to leave.

It turned out to be a little more challenging than I had first thought. Since I'm Presbyterian, it meant that I would have to graduate from high school, graduate from college, graduate from graduate school, take Hebrew and Greek, complete 2 internships, take five of the hardest ordination exams that even I could imagine, and then finally be considered "prepared" to become a minister.

Meanwhile, my Pentecostal friends were able to preach whenever the Spirit led them.

Perhaps my preaching philosophy of "Never Be Boring" seems a little too simple. Please don't get me wrong—it's not the only thing I tried to accomplish during a worship service. Of course, my first (and greatest) goal was to communicate the gospel of Christ. But because that falls in the "of course" category in my book, I didn't think it was all that necessary to list. My point is this: if you're boring, nobody will stay awake long enough to get it, anyway. And if you're boring, how will you ever get somebody excited about a relationship with the Lord?

I'm no longer a full-time pastor, but I still get to preach at church from time to time. So, even now, after many years, I try to stick to my "Never Be Boring" mantra.

As a result, when I look for sermon fodder, I've tried to take some of the more difficult Scripture passages, or cool doctrines of the church, or curious Bible figures, and turn them into sermon series that are both honoring to God and interesting to participate in.

Not always an easy task.

But that's where The Seven Deadly Sins come in. I find this ominous list particularly intriguing. Growing up, I never spent much time worrying about these Seven Biggies. I couldn't even name them…can you? At one point, I thought they maybe corresponded with the Seven Wonders of the World (which I also am unable to list), but apparently they are only similar in that they both have the number "seven" in their names. When the thought popped up that this might make a good sermon series, the pastoral team dove in. A decade or so and a lot of life, a lot of research, and a lot of writing later, I found I had enough material for seven volumes of books. I honed it down to what you are about to read.

In my mind, none of it has been boring.

I hope you feel the same.

ABOUT THE AUTHOR

Laurie Jackson is the Senior Director of Compass Care at Virginia Mason Memorial Hospital in Yakima, Washington. Compass Care is a service line that focuses on advancing illness and end-of-life care. She is also an ordained Presbyterian minister. After seminary, Laurie served full-time in churches from east coast to west coast before making the leap into healthcare. Her vision is to remove the fear of end of life throughout her community. In her work as a leader in hospice and palliative care, she has focused on advance care planning, primarily teaching on The Five Wishes (an advance directive that is currently legal in 42 states plus Washington, D.C.). She believes that we Christians have a unique opportunity to live our best lives because we have a peace that passes understanding in this world.

INTRODUCTION

Sin.

Let's be honest. You'd rather talk about sin than sit around chatting about saintliness.

Don't worry--it's not only you.

Who <u>doesn't</u> enjoy rubbernecking to see sin in action? As long as it's somebody else's sin, of course, and not yours.

You would think we'd grow tired of ambulance chasing to see how others messed up. But whenever there's a fall from grace or somebody lets the monster within come out, we seem to join the throngs to see what's going on.

From a distance, of course. No sense in getting too close.

Sin is nothing new. It didn't come about as a result of reality television, or the 60's, or Rock 'n Roll, or the turn of the century. Sin has been around since Adam & Eve thought the grass looked greener on the other side of the fruit.

The Seven Deadly Sins are nothing new, either. Apparently, there was a fourth-century Greek monastic theologian named Evagrius of Pontus. When he first drew up a list of eight offenses and wicked human passions, he couldn't have known how popular they might become in the next couple millennia. When Evagrius devised his offenses, he listed them in what he considered to be increasing ugliness: gluttony, lust, avarice, sadness, anger, acedia (that's Greek for "spiritual sloth"), vainglory, and pride.

Goofy list, huh?

Evagrius saw the increasing severity of each offense representing an increasing fixation on the self, finally ending with pride as the most egregious of the sins.

Since about the seventh century, the Church has used nearly the same list to denote the seven deadly sins. Thankfully for us, the Church combined and changed the names of a couple of the sins so we might actually know what sins we were committing. The "official" Seven Deadlies (although who actually presides over them is a little cloudy) are: pride, envy, gluttony, lust, anger, greed, and sloth.

Eeww.

Others have attempted to rank these sins according to seriousness or, like our boy Evagrius, to their increasing focus on the self. Pope Gregory the Great based his ranking on the degree from which each sin offended against love (but I'm not really sure about the scale he used). Later theologians, however, including St. Thomas Aquinas, would contradict the notion that the seriousness of the sins could be ranked in this or any other way.

In the end, the main point wasn't that one sin is greater than another, because, really, sin—any sin, whether it's that little white lie or one of the Deadlies—disconnects us from relationship with God. And that's bad. But the main point was—and still is—that these deadly sins are considered to be the big guys. They are dastardly demons that keep us from allowing God to be in control of our lives.

There's something more. We 21st-century Americans have an increasingly serious problem with the Seven Deadlies: we think either they're way out of reach, or way too dated—that they are so bad that "certainly *I* would never succumb to them," or way too obsolete to spend any time at all worrying about.

Don't be so sure. That's what I thought, too.

Our friend Evagrius, who came up with the list in the first place, lived through the Deadlies in a very personal way. Eventually, he got to a point where he realized that his life could change with being filled with the Spirit of God instead of being filled with deadly sin.

Go figure.

In the pages ahead, you will find that each chapter's subject matter is one of the Seven Deadly Sins. Each of the Deadlies begins with a passage from the Bible, which is referenced throughout the chapter. The sections within the chapters are snippits into daily life that relate to the respective sin of the chapter…and what to do about each one.

Enjoy your time reading about the Seven Deadly Sins—hopefully, even more than you would enjoy the momentary pleasure of partaking in the Deadlies themselves. And here, as you read, you can get pleasure without the guilt.

Dive into the Deadlies. You just might be surprised to find yourself somewhere in these pages.

ACKNOWLEDGMENTS

Dr. and Mrs. Samuel and Eileen Moffett, my uncle and aunt: I grew up with these two traveling home on furlough from Korea, where they were teaching and serving as missionaries during my early years. They later inspired me to attend Princeton Theological Seminary, where Uncle Sam served as the Henry Luce Professor of Mission and Ecumenics. Their love of people, love of the gospel, and love of writing helped me see that I, too, could share my memories with others. As Uncle Sam would regularly encourage others, saying, "Power to You," I, too, want to be an encouragement through my words and actions.

Bill and Maridean Bennett, my parents: I had no idea that my childhood was unique, mostly because it was what most today would call "normal." You raised us kids to love the Lord, love our family, and love each other. Thank you for being the best parents *ever*.

Steve Jackson, my husband: Every day with you has been a joy. I could not be more grateful to be your wife.

Ben and Mary Jo, my kids: Where did you come from?! You make me laugh, you make me proud. I have a Ben and Mary-sized place in my heart for you, always.

CHAPTER ONE: PRIDE COMETH BEFORE...WELL, YOU KNOW

PRIDE
WHO IS THE GREATEST?

Pride. What a sensational sin to begin with. What a terrific topic to study. How enlightening this will be. How entertaining. How helpful it will be for others to benefit from my work on the issue of pride.

Oh.

You've probably heard this before: "We often see in others what we don't want to see in ourselves."

If you've ever judged someone hastily, you may want to consider the appropriateness of this quote. It just may pertain to you like it all too often pertains to me.

"We often see in others what we don't want to see in ourselves."

The stumbling block of pride. It seems to be forever ready to wedge itself under the big toe and trip up whoever is closest to it. And oh, how easy it is to recognize this trip, this slip, this deadly sin…in somebody else.

But as often as it's hovering at the other end of the room, it's staring in the mirror as well.

Pride is prevalent in our world…and not just the "regular" world, but the "Christian" world as well. Maybe especially in the Christian world. As we start this little walk through the Deadlies together, I hope you'll be honest with yourself. I promise to do the same. I have the feeling I'm not the only one who struggles with this stumbling block. It's just that not many people want to admit that pride is a problem.

Including me.

Instead, we all seem to want to be better than that…and if we can't be that, at least we can be better than everyone else.

Check out this passage from chapter 9 of the Gospel of Mark (verses 33-37):

> *They came to Capernaum. When Jesus was in the house, he asked them, "What were you arguing about on the road?"*

But they kept quiet because on the way they had argued about who was the greatest. Sitting down, Jesus called the Twelve and said, "If anyone wants to be first, he must be the very last, and the servant of all." He took a little child and had him stand among them. Taking him in his arms, he said to them, "Whoever welcomes one of these little children in my name welcomes me; and whoever welcomes me does not welcome me but the one who sent me."

Can you believe those disciples? They're not very smart. Look at them, arguing with one another about which one is the greatest.

Even I am better than that.

Uh-oh.

It's surprising how quickly this issue of pride comes a-running. It's easy to look at the disciples and think that they're immature and that we would never do such a thing.

Silently, we could quite possibly be having the same sorts of arguments, but at least we wouldn't say the words out loud like they did.

The irony of it all is that pride typically comes, not out of competence or confidence, but out of their lack. In my lacking, I overcompensate, and—(*hack*)—there it is: that ugly pill of pride has just slid down my throat.

Have you ever noticed someone around you who is struggling with pride, and what you see isn't a lack of confidence, but just the opposite: overconfidence? Somebody who's watching a proud person might say, *Are they ever full of themselves! Nobody wants to be around a know-it-all.* And all the while, that person may not be trying to be the greatest; they're just wanting to be acknowledged for what they do know and have done, and not be considered the way they really feel: completely unsure of themselves.

A few years ago, I was serving as a pastor in a small church in north-central Ohio. I vividly recall the fateful day that I sat in my tiny office and prayed, "Lord, I'm ready to do ministry differently. I don't want acknowledgment for the things I've done. I want You—only You—to get the glory." Pretty good prayer, huh? Sounds like a normal kind of prayer for a Christian, or at least a pastor (forgive what sounds like pride here…it catches up with me in a moment, you'll see). Well, later that very day, a woman—a member of our church—came into my office and wedged herself into the tiny chair that barely fit in my closet/office. She told me that there was something she just had to share with me—something she felt had begun to change her life. The woman then proceeded to share a sermon she had recently heard. She could recite the whole thing—including the personal stories. The only problem was that she couldn't remember where she had heard the message. But, that wasn't a big deal, she said, because the messenger wasn't the most important thing—the <u>message</u> was.

I was the messenger.

Those were my stories. That was my sermon.

I was dying to say, "Wait! It's *me*! I said all those great things. I was the one who did all of that. Really, you can believe me, because I have the manuscript right here in my desk. It's me! It's me!"

And then that prayer came to me: "Lord, I want You—only You—to get the glory."

Oh. That's right.

I was surprised how hard it was for me to <u>not</u> take the credit. But when I take the credit, then God doesn't get it. I learned a difficult lesson that day…one that I am reminded of regularly.

The moment you start wanting just a little bit of acknowledgment, know this: pride is setting in. And pride always wants to feed the ego.

Pride sank its talons into the hearts of the disciples when they wanted to be recognized for all they had accomplished (in Jesus's name, of course. Yeah, right). They wanted someone to say, "Hey, you guys are pretty fantastic."

I want that, too.

Why is that necessary? Why is it important for us to stand out and be recognized as better than others? Even worse is when we lean toward the way of <u>false</u> humility, telling others that we aren't good enough, even when we firmly believe that we are, just so we will get the acknowledgment we so desperately long for.

There's barely a glance between confidence and pride, you know.

Humility and false humility are also only a blink apart. Whenever we start comparing ourselves, we're straying our vision toward the periphery instead of focusing straight ahead. When we are filled with pride, we are taking our eyes off the only One who has any right to compare, and we choose instead to look to ourselves, our accomplishments, our egos.

And that's when we typically blindside ourselves into pride.

Jesus continually reminds those who cross His path that life is not about them, their accumulation of goods, their talents, their wisdom, or their actions; it's about Him. True enjoyment comes in giving God glory. Real fulfillment is found when we use what He's given us and we see Him in those things.

Whether you are working, playing a sport, parenting, or just living, your focus is to be on Emmanuel—that means "God with us." Because He really is with you. And placing your eyes, your heart, and your vision on the Lord does something: all of a sudden, you discover that it doesn't matter if you're the greatest, because the Greatest is already here—with you, and in you.

And then, you have an opportunity for your heart and your actions to reflect that. When that happens, there's no need for pride or false humility, because life becomes about giving glory to God.

Take time today to look at Jesus first. May He bring you the perspective of who the greatest should actually be.

Then, you just might find yourself thinking: *Wow. Maybe this pride stuff was written for me to get a better handle on how to be humble.*

But don't forget: in truth…it was written for *me*.

PRIDE
LIVING LIFE UPSIDE-DOWN

A friend likes to say that "salad is not an entrée. It is simply a promise that the real food is on its way."

Maybe you feel similarly, not just about salad, but about the meal itself, that it is simply the bridge that one must cross in order to get to the Promised Land of dessert.

Ahh, dessert. Whether it's under-glass, on fire, or à la mode, just the thought of it makes me want to go to the fridge for a treat.

Some desserts look like art. Have you ever watched a cooking show or gone on a website or perused the magazine rack at the grocery store while you're waiting to check out and seen those intense and gorgeous works of art? Some of those desserts on the covers of those magazines look too beautiful to eat.

But I'm willing to take the challenge.

In the categories of Unique and Unusual, there's one dessert that tops them all. It isn't a fancy new dessert. It has no outrageous ingredients. And yet, when placed in the right combination, these ingredients come together and form something special: the pineapple upside-down cake.

Certainly, other desserts are more extravagant. Most sweets are visually more beautiful. But the beauty of the pineapple upside-down cake is not in the way it looks, or in the fluffy frosting that crowns it (since it doesn't even have frosting). No, the beauty of the pineapple upside-down cake is found in what's inside, when the goo that cooked on the bottom gets flipped to the top and oozes through the otherwise boring middle. In the pineapple upside-down cake, every forkful becomes the perfect bite, when the bottom becomes the top and the gooey ugliness becomes a thing of beauty.

Now, let's talk about the theology of the pineapple upside-down cake.

In many ways, what you just read as a description of a silly cake is a pretty good description of us human critters, too. All too often, we tend to praise--and judge--the things we see. But you already know that our best assets are found, not on top—on the surface—but within, deep below the exterior. Our personal character emanates not from perfectly glossed lips or a chiseled body or acne-free skin on the outside, but from a well-sanded soul that is found within.

People assess us by the words that we say, but those words are merely the fruit of the roots from which they come. When the heart is right, then the fruit is pure. When it's not, then what tends to come out is sour grapes.

For a moment, let's go back to our dessert. We're that cake. Think about it: like that pineapple concoction, we're really not that much to look at, if we are honest. The beauty of humans is what you can't see with the eyes—and that is truly upside-down to the world.

The problem is that, sometimes, something keeps us from being able to show who we really are. Sometimes we just can't make the flip and be the pineapple upside-down cake we were meant to be.

That something is pride.

I want to look different than I really am. I don't want to be a pineapple upside-down cake. I want to be an exotic and mysterious Framboise Flambé or Crème Brûlée or some other fabulous dessert that's impossible to pronounce, much less bake.

So I allow pride to interfere with who I really am.

On the road, Jesus asked the disciples what they were arguing about. They were, of course, fighting about who was the greatest—a ridiculous argument, to say the least. To nearly come to blows over who is more holy simply proves just how unholy the boys actually were. To try to convince anyone that I am most spiritual, most holy, most set apart by God only proves how very little I know about God, about what being holy means, and about myself.

Shame on them.

Shame on me.

…But I don't want to be a pineapple upside-down cake. I want to be a striking piece of Tiramisu.

Pride sets us apart from others in a completely different way than holiness does. Pride means "puffed up," and you can't very well walk alongside and listen to and share with others when you're puffed up. To be proud means to be "above" others, recognizing you are better than someone at something (even when you're not), whether it's something mental, physical, clinical, or social. When you are proud, you simply cannot remain on the same level as someone else.

And you make that choice yourself.

Holiness, however, is a little different. In its pure definition, the Greek word "holy" means "set apart." Here again, you aren't running with the pack, but you still remain on the same plane, the same level—not above (or below) anyone else—just called to be different. Removed. It's doesn't make you any better.

But it does make you His.

The problem for the disciples is that they were seeing holiness as an upgrade to a first-class ticket toward a four-star life, complete with being served, being respected, being revered. Jesus assured them that not only was this not the case, but they'd better get their aprons on, because it's time to start serving others.

In Mark 9:35, Jesus sat down. This was a sign that He was about to teach, and the disciples had better listen. Jesus called the Twelve and said, "If anyone wants to be first, he must be the very last, and the servant of all."

Did you see the pineapple upside-down cake flip just there?

You know, pineapple upside-down cake doesn't typically get a blue ribbon at a cake contest. I've never seen those celebrity chefs make a pineapple upside-down cake on their shows. Now: gorgeous wedding cakes, beautiful chocolate tortes, perfect parfaits? That's a different story. That's beauty in our world.

But Jesus is speaking to the Twelve.

Jesus is speaking to us.

He's speaking about a pineapple upside-down cake filled with the sort of true beauty that the world can't even see.

That's how Jesus gets to the core of who we really are.

The pineapple upside-down cake of your life is nothing if it doesn't get flipped. Maybe it's your fear of being rejected that keeps the cake in its pan. Maybe your life is staying where it is because you seem to think that even the side that's showing (the dry, boring side) is still better than everyone else's. Maybe you're letting your pride keep you where you are, by the words that you use or the actions that others see, and you don't even realize that your goo has gone nowhere.

Pride gets us stuck to our own sides instead of dripping out into a world that has never tasted the sweet, sweet love of Jesus.

It's time to make a change. It's time to let yourself be flipped. Let the mercy of God turn you into something that you never expected. Your outsides aren't the most important. What matters is what is in your heart.

Today, just for today, try working on being a person that is living inside-out, and upside-down from the way the world expects, and watch what happens.

You just might flip for Him.

PRIDE
WHO'S THE FAIREST?

She stands before the mirror every day. And every day, she asks the same question:

Mirror, Mirror, on the wall, who's the fairest of them all?

And, every day, she's expecting the same answer from this talking mirror: that she, of course, is the fairest, the most beautiful, the best of them all.

And that's the answer that she gets, every single day…right up until the day that someone fairer comes along.

What?? There's someone fairer, more beautiful, more perfect than I? I must destroy her at once!

Okay, now, let's back up for a moment. Anyone who needs a talking mirror to get an ego stroked clearly has more issues that ought to be addressed than wasting time trying to find a girl who lives with seven little men who whistle while they work.

And yet, short of the dwarves and the poison apple and all, are we really all that far from the wicked woman? We might not have a creepy talking mirror, but aren't we still looking for a particular response from a mirror, or the bathroom scales, or our families, or our friends? And when we don't get that response, instead of looking to ourselves, how many of us try to destroy the one close to us that is more fair?

Ouch. Little too close to home.

Pride sets in when we want to be the fairest. And it festers into bitterness when we realize we aren't. We want to be someone special to someone, if only to a mirror.

But if we don't feel special, unique, exotic, or mysterious, then envy, then discord, then anger, then wrath come out. These are sins that block us from being truly available to God. The more we want to be something for ourselves, the more we interfere with recognizing God's grace in our lives.

The Lord's mercy isn't lavished on us because we are the fairest, the strongest, or the best. In fact, just the opposite is true. God's grace, Jesus, came because He realized how wicked and wretched we really are. Pride sets in so easily for us. It feeds other sins like a breath of wind on a wildfire. God knows how we long to go to the mirror and be told we're the fairest, the best…or at least better than we think we are. But the moment that feeling of being good enough sets in, then we can't see grace. Grace reminds you that you don't have to be the fairest on earth to be valued, or the best in the world's eyes to be loved. God's grace covers you so that in His eyes, you already are the fairest you should be. And His eyes should be the only mirror that matters.

Proverbs 29:23 is a great one for this Deadly Sin: *A man's pride brings him low, but a man of lowly spirit gains honor.* Solomon reminds us that a humble heart gains satisfaction. A heart that cries out for mercy sees grace. The one who is allowed to be cracked open is the one who can be a servant of the Master.

If you go to the mirror to find success in yourself, you just may hear for a moment that you're better. But, just like the wicked witch, you will have to return every day. No matter how often you hear from others that you might actually be the fairest or the best, remember this: if that's what you're going for, then it will never be enough. You'll always be waiting for the day when you hear that someone else has taken the lead.

When we try to satisfy the soul with anything other than the One who made the soul, we will always come up short. Great joy comes in a gentle spirit and a humble heart.

Instead of trying to destroy somebody else so that you might lift yourself up, try humbling your heart…and letting the Lord take care of it. After all, He isn't into who the fairest is. In fact, He isn't even fair.

And we should be grateful for that…because grace isn't fair.

PRIDE
TOP THIS!

A few years ago, I took up racquetball with a girlfriend. We are actually tennis players, not racquetball players, and we looked a little goofy playing racquetball—okay, I looked a little goofy. I couldn't get the hang of it. Besides that, because we're so competitive, we both learned how to beat the tar out of the racquetball. Unfortunately, we were better at hitting each other with the ball, the racquets, the wall, the floor— you name it. After a couple of weeks into our new sport, we were both starting to look more like meatloaf than athletes.

One day, a guy at the athletic club walked by us as we were beating each other up—er, I mean, as we were playing racquetball. He wore a shirt with three words: "Chicks Dig Scars." As we read the shirt, we both agreed that the shirt speaks truth: we do dig scars. And in fact, if you're going to give me a scar, make it a good one that I can show off! From that point on, we felt as if we were validated (after all, it was on a shirt), and we've been beating each other up at every sport we play. When we're playing tennis, we don't try to miss the other person; instead, we try to hit each other, which does a couple of things: a) you win the point, and b) you just might get a bruise that you can show off.

And who doesn't want to show off a battle wound?

Certainly you've seen it happen: If one person starts to share a story surrounding how they broke their arm, you can bet that just around the bend is a better story from someone listening. *I can top that one.* Comments on cuts move to stories about scars which turn to battles about broken bones, then surgeries, then near-amputations and the like. We pretend that kids are the only ones trying to one-up each other, but as adults, we do it even more…just a little more subtly.

Sometimes.

You know people that want to be the center of a conversation. One person says something, and the other wants to jump in with another fact, and so on and so on. Whose head is filled with the most useless trivia? Who is the best story teller? Who is the greatest jokester? Pretty soon, they're all scratching their way to the top, wanting to be the main attraction.

In this chapter's Bible passage, God was in conversation with the Twelve. God—that's who Jesus was and is. If anyone commands respect and warrants our attention, it's God Himself.

Jesus entered the room. And the disciples, instead of focusing on Jesus, began to argue about which of them is the greatest. They, too, liked to play the "Top This" game. They were spending more time looking to themselves rather than to the love that Jesus so desperately wanted to shower on them.

Pride gets in the way of our being the servants that God wants us to be, too.

When I play the "Top This" game, then I take my eyes off the Lord and put them onto myself...which is a surprisingly easy thing to do. Seeing myself then becomes much more important than looking to Jesus.

I used to teach G.E.D. preparation classes to teenage students here in town. Gang members, pregnant teens, and kids in difficult home and life situations made up the majority of my class; most had either been kicked out of or quit school. I helped get them ready to take the high school equivalency test.

But as I look back, I realize they were often teaching me more than I was teaching them.

One of the games a particular class of mine used to play during breaks was "Top This...Body-Marking-Style." For a number of weeks, my students made a game of trying to get the best body piercing, or the best tattoo—a permanent mark on the body—in order to one-up a classmate. The young man that ended the game came in one evening with a large piece of gauze taped to his shoulder. The weekend before, he had been *branded*. Just like steer on a ranch. Game over—nobody wanted to top that. You would have thought the young man had earned an Academy award...not a permanent scar. But to him, this brand marked him as the best, at the top of the heap.

> Look at verse 35: *If anyone wants to be first, he must be the very last, and the servant of all.*

A friend in grad school was one of those men who will always look young. In his mid-thirties at the time, he could convince anyone he was no more than about 20. He looked like one of those innocent young men that can do no wrong. The fact that he was the son of a minister added weight to that innocence. As I recall him telling the story, he came home from college one summer after having a revelation. The year before, while he was away at school, he had read in his Bible the passage in Deuteronomy 15 about a servant that doesn't want to leave his master; a sign of his commitment is to push an awl through the earlobe. My friend decided to do something similar: get his ear pierced for the Lord. Then he declared to God that if anyone asked him what the earring was for, he would say that it was because he was marked as a slave for the Lord.

Now, plenty of people get earrings. But this particular piece of jewelry looked completely out of place attached to this young man's lobe.

Apparently, the little earring caused a stir. It started to become a great tool for this young man to share his faith…right up until Mr. Clean-Cut went home for the summer and got a job at the local mill, where he was the smallest employee, and a newbie, surrounded by rough-and-tumble workers who had been there for years. He was sure he was going to die (or be killed) the moment he entered with his cute, little earring.

On the first day, he made it very few steps into the building before he was confronted. "Whatcha doin' with that sissy earring, Boy??"

He stopped cold in his tracks. This was the moment of truth. During the pregnant pause, as the blood drained from his extremities, he had to choose what to do. Quickly, he figured that he'd be entering heaven any moment anyway, so he might as well honor the commitment he'd made. He looked up to Goliath and replied, "I, er, I've been, uh, mar—mar—marked as a slave for God."

And then he cringed, waiting to get pummeled.

The pummeling never came.

By the end of the summer, this young man was leading a Bible study with a number of his new friends in the mill.

It's pretty difficult to be a self-centered servant. By definition, a servant is a slave, commanded to seek out the interest of the one he is serving. To be a self-centered servant—well, that's really an oxymoron, because a self-centered servant won't make it very long.

Jesus didn't play Top This. Instead, Jesus was humble in such a way that others might come to be captured by Him, not His suave godliness. His true character was shown in His commitment to being a servant to humans (completely the opposite of the way it "should" be).

Pride keeps us from being all that God wants us to be. True medicine for us is to fall to our knees and take a big dose of humility. When we feel we are last is when we are right where The Lord wants us...and can use us best.

If the human race were truly a race, Jesus wouldn't be in the front of the pack, crossing the finish line in record time. No, He'd be back in the pack, encouraging others, not narrowly focused on His own ability but on the strengths of those he's running with as they trudge along.

I want to have the kind of humility that helps others see Jesus. He, not I, should be at the top.

PRIDE
GLAD I'M NOT LIKE HIM

Let's talk about something purely hypothetical, something that would never happen in this day and age. Turn in your Bible to the Gospel of Luke, chapter 18. In this chapter, Jesus tells some parables (a parable is a story with a point behind the plot). One of the parables is about a Pharisee and a Tax Collector. Here's the scene, as Jesus describes it (beginning at verse 10):

> *Two men went up to the temple to pray, one a Pharisee and the other a tax collector. The Pharisee stood up and prayed about himself: "God, I thank you that I am not like other men—robbers, evildoers, adulterers—or even like this tax collector. I fast twice a week and give a tenth of all I get."*

Get the picture? This is a pride-filled man. There's no question about it, right? You'd think so. But the fact is that the Pharisee would probably not agree he's being proud. The reality is that this man probably sees himself as humble; after all, he's coming to the temple to pray, and that's not a proud thing, right?

Right?

It's fascinating how close the distance is between humility and pride. The Pharisee saw himself as different from the others. He was a lawyer of the church, a man of God, a person obedient to the Law; if anyone had a right to look down on others, he certainly did.

But he was looking in the wrong direction. That's because no person has the right to look down on another. The moment we look away from Christ and toward ourselves, the best we can hope for is a sense of false humility.

The Pharisee saw himself as humble because he prayed and fasted and tithed. But God saw him as proud. Jesus then compared this man, the holy Pharisee, to the tax collector (verse 13):

But the tax collector stood at a distance. He would not even look up to heaven, but beat his breast and said, "God, have mercy on me, a sinner."

The tax collector wouldn't even look heavenward, because he knew that his heart was so full of sin that he wasn't worthy. The tax collector cried out, "Have mercy."

The great thing about the tax collector is that he knew he did nothing right. He knew he was a sinner. He knew he had to rely on God's mercy.

Pride can be so subtle—even (and sometimes especially) in the church. With a little nudge, though, pride can blow up as big as a hot-air balloon. That false humility can become the very air that lifts us into thinking we're greater than others.

But the tax collector didn't...couldn't...lift himself up. He was down too far. So he did the only thing left for him to do: lift the Lord up. The tax collector realized that only through God's mercy could he become a servant of the King. Like the Pharisee and the tax collector, we, too have a choice: we can serve to make God look good, or we can keep trying to push everyone else down in order to make ourselves look good.

A few years ago, my aunt and uncle were invited to an event at Buckingham Palace—quite an honor. Before they headed "across the pond," they were given a list of etiquette dos and don'ts for while in the palace. Following are a few of the many points of etiquette they were required to follow (and remember):

- Women should curtsy; men can nod their heads. Americans, however, are not required to bow or curtsy before British royalty.
- Do not touch any member of the royal family, unless they touch you first.
- Royals proffer their hands first, and handshakes should be short and not too hard. Avoid turning your back on the queen unless it can't be helped.

There can feel such a chasm between royalty and the rest of us. They seem to be on an entirely different level than us "normal" folk, even though modern kings and queens are simply humans that got lucky enough to be born into a particular family.

Now consider Jesus, the King of Kings and Lord of Lords.

What's your attitude when you come before Him? What's your gauge? Think about this: how many times have you fallen asleep while talking with the Lord? Can you count how often you've been praying and you've gotten distracted by a phone call, or a commercial, or a text?

It's easy to look at the stuff that we do and think we're pretty humble. It's easy to look at the stuff we see others do and see how humble they <u>aren't</u>. And that's when our pride begins to puff us up and lift us higher.

May God have mercy on us in our pride. May God have mercy on us whenever we think we are actually worthy of His love. May God have mercy upon you whenever you think you're good enough to deserve to enter Heaven's gates. May God have mercy upon me when I feel like I'm better than anyone else.

As with the disciples, God's never going to compliment you on how humble you are. You can never be too humble. In fact, maybe we can never be humble enough. And God won't lie and tell us that we're doing great—because that would probably result in pride, which would prove how great we're not.

But there is something even greater that He will do: tell you how loved you are.

Because you are.

PRIDE
TOO GOOD FOR THE DOG

Nigel was a 7-year-old Welsh Corgi. A Welsh Corgi is a dog unlike any other dog. Well, actually, you've probably seen parts of a Welsh Corgi in other dogs. They're the goofiest things—picture this: a German Shepherd body; enormous paws on the ends of surprisingly short legs; a long, furry tail; and gigantic ears.

Curiously, Nigel was an extremely serious dog. Unfortunately, nobody that looked at him could be serious.

Nigel knew his job, and he followed it with every fiber of his fur. It was his responsibility to be sure the family stayed safe. He would case the perimeter of the property like any good soldier. Nigel was a great doorbell, announcing the presence of all humans (and most critters) onto the property. He actually alerted us three separate times when people accidentally ran their car into our ditch out in the front of our property (we lived in the country). He was a self-feeder (which means you could leave a bowl of food on the floor and he would eat only until he got full). He followed us outside and onto the lawn without a leash (or the safety of a fence). He was an overall good dog.

Until the day that I got home from work and found Nigel sleeping a little too soundly on the floor in the hallway. We buried him in the backyard, and we swore he would never get another dog.

Three weeks later, Thomas, another Corgi, hopped out of the car and into our lives.

Thomas was arguably the happiest-looking dog in at least the western hemisphere. From the chest up, the old dog Nigel had looked regal; from the old dog's stature, it was easy to see why The Queen of England has Corgis herself. But where Nigel looked like royalty, Thomas looked like a cartoon. His body was almost entirely black, except for his paws, his nose, and the tip of his tail, all of which were white. I know, he still sounds pretty good. The problem—problems, I should say—come in placement and size. His black ears rivalled Dumbo's. His paws looked less like they belong on a dog and more like they should be on a bear (as a puppy, he would soak his paws in his water dish when he got too hot). His tongue was too large and didn't fit in his mouth, so it would frequently hang out the side of his face, giving him a Dopey quality (again, less than regal). His legs, if you can believe it, were shorter than those of a regular Corgi, and his body was larger, topping out at 48 pounds—he could high-center on a sock. And that tail: with that white end, it's as if it glowed in the dark. And that wouldn't be that bad, except that Thomas only wagged his tail...vertically.

Up and down.

And when he was really happy, his wag would beat on the floor like a drum.

If you wanted him to drop whatever was in his mouth, you used the obvious command, "Sit."

Of course, there was no real reason for him to actually sit. You couldn't really tell when he was obeying, anyway.

His favorite chew toy was a piece of his own poop.

And every one of my right shoes.

Well, not every one. Only the dressy ones. He preferred heels.

And books, but, again, only mine. He chewed up one Bible, two daily devotionals, and a Bible dictionary. Hopefully, he got something out of them.

In short, he was a menace. And I'm not a bit afraid to share how I feel. Thomas was not well potty-trained ("But, Laurie, he *goes* in the bathroom. Sure, it's on the bathmat, but that's pretty good, don't you think? In fact, it's almost impressive"). His teeth should have been registered with Hewlett-Packard as shredding devices. He didn't ever alert us when someone came onto the property—but his ear-piercing barker wouldn't stop if he saw two people hug and he wasn't one of the people.

Then there was the day that he swallowed 60 feet of dental floss. He had emergency surgery, where the vet opened up his stomach and intestines in seven places. We started calling him "Spring Break," because he cost us our family vacation that spring. I was only slightly comforted when we visited Thomas at the veterinarian intensive care and saw that he had to wear the "cone of shame" (because he had chewed up his catheter). He deserved the cone. Wish I had one for him at home.

Oh, and he healed just fine.

Unfortunately.

I couldn't stand that dog. And I couldn't stand that he was so cute that he got away with every obnoxious thing he did. Every week, he added hours more work to my life. I longed for the day when someone could say that they rescued him from the pound. I wished we would never have gotten him …

Until the day I saw the mouse.

It was belly-up, right next to Thomas, who was sitting at attention (I think he was sitting—back to the whole "no legs" thing), waiting for me to notice his new buddy. I could practically see the thought bubble swirling over Thomas' head: "Mom, he's super-cute, isn't he? He's my new friend. Want me to toss him to you? All I have to do is pick him up in my teeth like this, and…"

"No, Thomas!"

Later that evening, Thomas found his new buddy's buddy. And we found that buddy in his teeth, too.

And all of a sudden, Thomas had a purpose. And Thomas became cuter. And I wanted him around.

When Thomas didn't serve my needs, when he was useless to me, then I simply considered him useless for living. But once he became the mighty mouse hunter, I recognized that he could do things that I couldn't do.

And I decided to love him.

Too bad I didn't just love him unconditionally from the start.

I wonder how I would feel if someone treated me that way.

Of course, I'm sure you would never treat another *human* the way I've acted concerning my dog. I'm sure that I never would.

Sure.

PRIDE

CAUGHT PRIDE-HANDED

Scene: Mom and 8-year-old son, Ben, on their way to school.

(Mom): So, Ben, have you decided what you want to be when you grow up?

(Ben): Mom, I've told you like a hundred times already. I am *going* to be an author, just like you…

(Mom begins to beam with pride)

(Ben): Except I'm going to be a *lot* more famous.

(Pride goes down the drain, Mom is devastated, sorry she packed great lunch for son.)

Why did that bother me so much? Was it that he doesn't understand the complexity of my responsibilities? Perhaps. Was it that I know how tough it is to get published, and it takes more than just good words to make a living writing? Perhaps. Was it that he was probably right, and I'd like to think of myself as better than I actually am?

Gulp.

Pride comes in a variety of packages. Even when we think we're being humble, we can turn the tide of pride to ourselves…and hardly notice we did it.

It starts with the best of intentions. I want to serve the Lord, and I want to find the perfect Scripture passage to confirm my service. Take Philippians 4:13:

I can do all things through Him who gives me strength.

This is a Christ-focused phrase. Because of the power that only Jesus can give, all things are possible. I should not doubt or question what the Lord may have in store for me, if I will recognize that He is infusing me with His strength.

And in a flash, I can turn this Jesus-centered vision of what humans can do when they are being steered by the Lord into a statement that is dripping with personal pride.

I can do all things. In fact, I can do anything. And if I find there's something that I'm not able to do, well, that's God's fault, not mine.

On the other hand, when I actually do accomplish something, well, then, kudos to me. After all, I'm the one who has had to make the sacrifice. After all, I'm the one who has had to show the discipline and the motivation. After all, it was my brain that cooked it up. Sure, I'll tell people, "All glory to God," and I mean it...but I need a little crumb myself. After all, if it weren't for me, it wouldn't have been accomplished.

How quickly I forget Jesus's words to us. His words are simple. His words are true.

Apart from me you can do nothing (John 15:5).

What are you doing right now? What project are you in the middle of...and why? Does that thing, whatever it is, make you look good, or does it make God look good?

The opposite of pride is humility. You already know that. One of the best ways of showing humility is through honesty and vulnerability.

Are you trying to put on a face that isn't your own? Are you working hard to be something other than the pineapple upside-down cake that you were created to be? Are you trying like anything to justify your behavior at work, or in the church, or at home, because you are following all the rules...unlike that sinner over there?

A counseling/consulting/publishing group called Syque helps people understand how we can come to see our own behavior versus how we see others'. They describe it this way: "We see others' behavior caused by disposition, ours by situation."

Read it again. Doesn't that make crazy sense? Others--they are the way they are because of who they are. My problems, meanwhile, lie in the circumstances I've been handed, and I can excuse my wrongs, because I understand what has happened to me. They, on the other hand...they're in TROUBLE.

In the end, do you find you give yourself more grace than you give others? Like that quote from Syque, it's mostly because we understand our situation and only think we understand others' situations. It certainly makes sense that our pride could be greatly diminished if we would work to listen to others, turn away from ourselves and fix our eyes on the cross, and remember that we were created as beings of worship... not beings of worry.

Quit worrying. Easier said than done, isn't it? Remember: Philippians 4 is a reminder that I don't have to worry. *Be anxious for nothing*, Paul tells the church in Philippi. Don't even be anxious that you're going to get what's coming to you. You don't have to worry.

Ultimately, pride comes out of some sort of fear. Maybe it's a fear that you won't be appreciated. Maybe it's a fear that you'll be seen for who you actually are. Maybe it's a fear that the truth about you really will come out.

Here's the truth: you ARE appreciated. You are deeply loved. The Lord Himself came to the earth, and He lived here for you. He walked the path to the cross for you. He died for you. And He rose again so that you could give your heart to Him and serve Him with joy, with thanksgiving, with humility. Now that's a great life.

The only One who matters already knows you...and knows you even better than you know yourself. On this day, at this hour, right this very minute, stop everything else and relax. There is nothing in life that is greater than the Lord, and He knows you, He knows what you need, and He knows what you don't.

Take heart as your soul soaks in more of Philippians 4:

> *Rejoice in the Lord always. I will say it again: Rejoice! Let your gentleness be evident to all. The Lord is near. Do not be anxious about anything, but in everything, by prayer and petition, with thanksgiving, present your requests to God. And the peace of God, which transcends all understanding, will guard your hearts and your minds in Christ Jesus.*

Finally, brothers, whatever is true, whatever is noble, whatever is right, whatever is pure, whatever is lovely, whatever is admirable—if anything is excellent or praiseworthy—think about such things.

Whatever you have learned or received or heard from me, or seen in me—put it into practice. And the God of peace will be with you.

He is.

PRIDE
SUPER POWER

They say we each have a super-power. By "they," I mean the boys in my family (they've also been watching far too many movies, so that's probably where their thinking came from. I keep trying to tell them that movies aren't real, but they scoff at me like I just said something insane).

Mary Jo, the youngest in our family, is considered "The Brain"— she's crazy smart. I guess I'm thankful for this nickname, because an older brother could easily have decided she had a different super-power and then dubbed his sister something much more obnoxious.

I am called "The Voice of Doom"—I'm not really sure about the etymology of my nickname. Perhaps it's from working in hospice for so many years, but I'm guessing it's actually because I'm the only one that makes sure the kids do their chores before they watch television. How that translates into a super-power, I'm not sure, but I'm willing to go with it.

Thomas, the dog, is an overachiever in the gas department (we call it "honking"). He has actually been known to be sound sleep, belly-up, and then honked so loudly that he's startled himself awake and then run right into the wall before recognizing what he's done.

We're so proud.

My husband Steve's super-power is barbecue sauce. Maybe that doesn't sound like a super-power to you, but the extent to which he utilizes puréed tomatoes is impressive. He puts barbecue sauce on nearly everything. And not just a little sauce, either; by the time by the time the meal is *over*, he still has a pool of it on his plate (and the placemat, and often the surrounding tablecloth).

Meanwhile Ben, when a teenager, really had the unmatched super-power. It was impressive. It was obvious. We all bowed to it.

He had the super-power of stink.

And I couldn't figure out where it came from.

You could walk down the hall, whistling a happy tune, and be completely knocked over by the wall of stink that hits you 18-inches before his bedroom door.

The room smelled like the insides of sneakers after a 15-year-old has worn them, without socks, while traipsing around a muddy fishing hole all day and then walking home (with the dead fish remaining in the shoes). I used tongs to remove his shoes from his room and air them out. I made sure he did his laundry regularly (and watched to see that he's using the right amount of laundry detergent...plus a couple extra fabric softener sheets for good measure). I didn't let him eat in his room. He showered every day, and he used deodorant as frequently as I reminded him (Ben, it's been an hour. Go put some on).

I regularly convinced myself that there must be something dead in there.

So, I checked under the bed. Nope, nothing but old homework assignments he forgot to turn in. The only thing in the closet was one lone pair of dress slacks that I hung up months before (I think Ben was afraid that hanging up his clothes would somehow alter his chemical makeup and make him less cool...or whatever term they're using these days).

Even the dog has stopped coming in—and that's impressive, because, as you know, Thomas (the dog) had been known to eat his own poop and roll in the remains of week-old dead birds.

I plead with him. The stink remained. I punished him. The smell was still there. I fumigated the room with professional strength air cleaners. But no use. I wouldn't let his friends enter the coned-off area (because, really, would you do that to a friend?). And yet, I couldn't fully get rid of the stench.

It finally dawned on me that the only person Ben's super-power was really bothering...was me. I didn't want friends or neighbors or teachers to think that I was a bad parent because I allowed my son to stew in his own stench and then step out of the house without worrying about his aroma. I was concerned that company would think I was less than Martha Stewart because a portion of our home needed to be quarantined due to the odor. In the end, I was the one with the real problem, not Ben.

Want to know how Ben's super-power started to diminish?

He started to like girls…and worry about how he smelled around them.

Now we have masculine-scented soap, and shampoo, and conditioner (I didn't know he even knew what conditioner was!). He can be seen at home, walking around rubbing his chin, saying that his manly beard is starting to come in—and then he likes to show us his whisker.

Yup, that was singular.

His previous pride over his super-power of stink has shifted into a pride in hygiene…and I couldn't be more grateful. But it has taken me getting off my own high horse in order to see that I don't have control over every little thing; if I'd just relax a little, I might actually remember those words from Jeremiah 29:11—

> *For I know the plans I have for you," declares the LORD,*
> *"plans to prosper you and not to harm you, plans to give*
> *you hope and a future."*

And I might add: *plans to give you a home without stench, and plans to prosper your son and help him have priorities other than his super-power of stink.*

Too bad it always takes me just a little too long to recognize that God knows what He's doing.

I'd save myself a lot of time.

PRIDE
KNOWLEDGE IS POWER

I can't tell you how many times I've gotten phone calls or e-mails from friends who were somewhere and needed the answer to some inane trivia question, so of course they thought I would know it. I can tell you that my ability to recall random information brings me more than just a little satisfaction. After all, didn't Schoolhouse Rock, that wonderful television teaching tool from the 1970s, teach us that *Knowledge is Power*? Unfortunately, there's that little quote from Lord Acton in 1877 that's also true: *Power corrupts...and absolute power corrupts absolutely.*

That second one's not my favorite quote.

I love to know things. I love to teach others stuff that they can, in turn, share with others. But sometimes, I'm the one who ends up getting the lesson.

Take, for example, one winter Sunday morning in worship. It was a Communion Sunday, and, as a pastor, I was up in the front presiding over the sacrament. My son Ben was eight years old at the time, and, for some reason, he was sitting alone in the pew.

Okay, so Ben is sitting alone. And it comes time for Communion. In that church, we took Communion by passing the trays of bread and juice down the aisles: this meant that you would take a piece of bread from the tray, and eat it when you're ready; and then, when the next tray came around, you'd take a mini shot-glass of grape juice and hold it until everybody had been served, then drink the juice together.

In this particular church, the bread was made a special way. The deacons had not used regular bread. Instead, they had taken store-bought pie crust dough—you know, the one that comes in a can and pops when you're least expecting it—and cut it into squares, so the "bread" absolutely melted in your mouth. Oh, the Body of Christ in that church, it was delicious.

It wasn't until it was time to serve Communion that I realized Ben was by himself. In our church, the only requirements for taking Communion are accepting Jesus Christ as your Lord and Savior, and having been baptized. Typically, our students went through a Confirmation class before they took Communion, but it's not a requirement. So, while there wasn't an adult he knew in his vicinity when Communion started, I wasn't worried that Ben would be able to figure it out.

Because I am so awfully spiritual and always focused on the important things, at that moment I was focused on my exciting trivia: I really wanted him to know that the bread was actually pie crust.

So, after worship, I walked straight up to Ben, who was still sitting in the pew. I plopped down next to him. I hadn't been able to see if he had taken Communion during the service, so I asked him if he had.

His response: "Yup."

I was super excited to share my wisdom about the pie crust with him.

"Did you like the bread?"

"Yeah, it was okay."

"Do you know what it was made of?"

That's when Ben, squirrelly little kid that he could often be, stopped everything. He stood up, and he looked me straight in the eye.

"Of course I know what the bread was made out of," he chastised. Then he said the best word I think I've ever heard.

"Manna."

And he walked away to find the rest of the family.

He must be so used to me quizzing him. He knows that "every moment is a teachable moment" (I apparently say that a lot). He knew the story about God providing the Israelites with manna, and, while he maybe didn't get the story exactly right, he certainly taught me that he's been paying attention, and he knows that God is providing for us, even today.

Oh, to have the faith of a child.

I was definitely put in my place that morning...by an eight-year-old. Ben reminded me that the stories in the Bible are not just stories from hundreds (or even thousands) of years ago. They matter right now.

Ben helped me get away from my know-it-all attitude, if only for a moment, to recognize that God knows more than I do.

Truth be told, sometimes even an 8-year-old does.

PRIDE

MacGuyver

I used to really like the television show "MacGuyver"—the original one. It was a typical 80s show, because MacGuyver was the good guy that always got the bad guy; but that wasn't the great part of the show. The best part was that this guy knew how to get himself out of jam after jam, because he could take what was around him and build something that would help him escape his precarious situation.

And what was great was what he would build. MacGuyver could turn a bedsheet and two paper clips into a 4-passenger airplane. He could take a balloon, a broken chair, and a feather, and turn it into an oxygen tank that would sustain him underwater for exactly the forty-two and a half minutes that he needed.

This guy was my hero.

I've always fancied myself as MacGuyver-esque. I like to think that I can take ordinary things and make them into the extraordinary. Unfortunately, my ability to do that has actually never materialized beyond my own mind.

So, one late spring weekend, I had come upon a great used gas barbecue, a real find—and perfect because we loved to have people over but always seemed to run out of room on our regular barbecue. It came with the tubing to attach the propane tank to the unit, but, for some reason, try as I might, I couldn't get the tubing to connect to the propane tank correctly.

I needed a new hose, or an adaptor, or something.

I can do that, I thought. After all, I'm MacGuyver. This should be an easy task.

Now, it just so happened that all the men in my life were at a men's retreat on this particular weekend. But hey, I didn't need them, I told myself.

I knew that, if it was to be, it would be up to me.

I was ready for the challenge. And I was already beginning to well up with pride.

First, I got down on the ground to look at where the hose should be connected. Sure, I didn't really have a clue what I was looking at or looking for, but I did get a nice spot of grease on my jeans from the ground, so I was already feeling pretty tough and proud. I found the outlet, but no matter how hard I tried to get the fitting to connect to the tank, I could not get them together.

Finally, deciding that there was no other way than to get help, I headed down to the hardware store and see if I could get the proper hose—or adaptor—or whatever—so that I could get my barbecue working. I figured there would be some MacGuyver-type men working there, so that seemed a reasonable place to go.

And, once I got to the hardware store, I could see there were a number of other MacGuyvers there, so I headed toward one. But just as I walked past the wrench aisle, a woman employee walked up to me and asked if she could help me.

I really didn't think so.

I didn't want to embarrass her, so my mouth said, "Well, maybe you can help me," but my mind said, "Mmmm, I doubt it." After all, she did not look like she had the MacGuyver quality I was looking for.

Clearly, this task would be beyond her ability.

However, being a person of extreme grace and mercy, I decided to give her a chance. I took out the hose, and I showed this non-Macguyver clerk the problem. "I can't get this end of the hose to fit correctly on my propane tank," I explained in clear and easy terms, showing her the fitting and the hose, which I knew that she would need to see for just this illustration. Slowly, I asked, "Maybe you could find someone that might be able to help me." I wanted her to not feel bad just because she couldn't handle something so difficult.

She looked at me kindly, almost as if she really appreciated the grace I was giving her. She then gently reached for the hose. First, she took the end that I had been trying all morning to go into the fitting of the propane tank, and she set that end down and grabbed the OTHER end of the hose, immediately screwing it into the propane tank sitting next to us. And, of course, it fit perfectly.

All morning, I had been trying to fit the wrong end of the hose onto the propane tank.

And here was the kicker. She didn't give me the look I was expecting—you know, the look I would have given her if I had just shown her that I was MacGuyver and she wasn't. So, I said the only thing that I could say.

"Uh, and I'd like a tank of propane, too, if it isn't too much trouble."

She bled the propane tank, she filled it with 4¼ gallons of propane, she rang me up, and then she waited for me to pay because I had dropped my wallet somewhere along the way and had to retrace my steps in search of it. As I was looking for it, I figured that some other MacGuyver had probably found my wallet and turned it into a boat.

Oh, I learned so much that day. I learned that nothing is ever as easy as I think it's going to be. I learned that no matter how hard I try to jam the wrong thing into the wrong fitting, I'm not going to make it work right.

But mostly, on that hot Saturday morning, I learned how proud I am, and how humble God would prefer I be.

That's being humbled. The difference between being humbled and intentionally humbling myself is this: that whole morning was an example of being humbled. Humbling myself…is telling you the story.

I am becoming more and more convinced that God does not want to humble us…but He does give us plenty of opportunities to humble ourselves.

I get myself into predicaments pretty often. I typically try to scoop up my pride and act as if nothing happened. But humbling myself is a whole different ballgame.

The word "humble" is found 71 times in Scripture, but what came to my mind that day at the hardware store was James 4:10:

Humble yourselves before the Lord, and he will lift you up."

He's ready to lift you up. Are you ready to humble yourself before Him?

PRIDE
A TEACHABLE MOMENT

The kids Wednesday after-school program at our church was a big hit in my family. My two kids seemed to enjoy the Bible time, they liked the snacks, they sang out loud, and they played great games. But, at least in my house, the conversation after we got home on Wednesday evenings typically focused on the dinner that we had at church that evening. Interestingly enough, we rarely talked about the food. Usually, we talked about the goofy person up at the front who was dressed up in a purple cape, a silly crown, and strangely clown-like hair: the Dinner Queen.

Also known to my children as *Mom*.

"Mom, why did you tell such goofy stories during dinner tonight?"

"Mom, what was that weird song you sang?"

"Mom, why can't we call you the Dinner Queen when we're outside of the kids program?"

"Mom, why do people look at you and laugh?"

That last one doesn't always coincide with me being the Dinner Queen.

One night, after the program, we were heading home in the dark of night (6:35 p.m. in November), and my 8-year-old, Ben, started asking about the prayer that we say before dinner. Finally, I thought, an intelligent, perhaps theological conversation is about to begin.

"Mom, when we pray before dinner at church, you always make us end the prayer with that Lord's Prayer thing. That's cool. I like it when we all pray together."

That's my boy.

"It's just, well, I have a question. I thought God was in heaven. But you keep saying that He's not. I don't get it."

Thinking that we were about to embark on a deep study of the Trinity, where Jesus sits at the right hand of God the Father and the Holy Spirit dwells within our hearts, I started to get really excited. But

34

then, I thought I'd better get a little clarification first. So, I asked Ben why he thinks that I keep saying that God's not in heaven.

Ben replied, "Because you make us all say, 'Our Father, who aren't in heaven...'"

Oops.

Ben and I ended up having a wonderful talk about what the Lord's Prayer means. We spent following conversations working through the words in the Bible (you can find it in Matthew 6:9-13). It opened up a whole new world for a young man in the next generation. And it was one more thing that brought my son and me closer.

Maybe you have lots of traditions. Perhaps you have words or phrases that you can recite for memory but your little ones may be hearing for the first time. Take a moment to share why you do what you do. Find Jesus in the experience. Teach your kids, and their kids, about the importance of what the Lord has done for you...and for them.

And be ready for more questions. You have an opportunity to teach them about what you believe...no matter how trivial you think the subject matter is.

After all, I never thought that being the Dinner Queen at a Wednesday after-school program could be such an important and spiritual part of their lives.

PRIDE
GIVING THANKS...NO MATTER WHAT

Okay, I admit it. The only thing I want to be (more than exotic and mysterious, of course, but that should go without saying) is impressive. I want to look good—like I am the Enjoli woman who can "bring home the bacon—da-na, na-na—fry it up in the pan—da-na, na-na—and never, never, ever let you forget you're a man"...sort of a contemporary Proverbs 31 woman. I'd like to think I am a combination of Martha Stewart and MacGuyver, who could build a table and chairs to seat 20, and then cook a meal worthy of a magazine cover.

But it never seems to work out that way.

Take a Thanksgiving not so long ago.

Ahh, Thanksgiving. A time for family. A time for fun. In my house, it means a time for way too much food, and football...and foibles.

It was my first year to host my side of the family, which meant a party of 19 for the day. Knowing how we all seem to have the spiritual gift of eating, I wanted to make sure that this year I would be the ultimate hostess, prepared with plenty of provisions for an afternoon of engorgement. We began at noon with ping-pong and appetizers. By the time the family began to arrive, I had already prepared the two 20-pound turkeys and set them in the two electric roasters I had placed on the counter.

Unfortunately, I didn't know how to use the electric roasters. The birds were pretty big, so I thought I should take out the insert from each roaster. Once the smoke began to billow from the roaster, I realized that was perhaps a poor idea. Then I called a friend who is much more qualified in the kitchen than I. This friend suggested that I put water in the bottom part of the roaster. That also turned out to be less than ideal, because once the water began to boil it started to shoot out from the crack between the roaster and the lid.

By this time, I decided to go straight to the top: I called two of the elderly ladies of the church, who got me back on pace for a three-thirty dinner. Bird 1 that had a nice crust from the first parching, and the near-smoking early on seemed to be cooking wonderfully once two o'clock rolled around. But Turkey 2 was struggling to even get warm. Great, I thought, I'm going to be in trouble.

I wanted to be sure there was enough food, so to the two turkeys I quickly added a pork roast.

Knowing that the pork roast is supposed to take only about an hour and a half, I thought I'd get started on it early. I got out my cool new electric grill (so that my pint-sized oven could be available for such things as burning the mashed potatoes in record time or for the sweet potatoes that I didn't know how to cook), and I plugged the grill into the outlet.

Nothing.

No heat from the grill element. No current from the cord. No shock as I grabbed the end of the cord with my wet hand.

Nothing.

Now I was in some serious trouble. I had one smoking turkey, one raw turkey, and one giant tree-trunk of a pork roast that wasn't cooking.

At about 3:30, I realized that I had blown a fuse in the kitchen, which affected only the outlets, and which explained why Turkey 2 wasn't cooking. It also explained why the electric grill didn't work, but I was beyond dealing with the pork roast—after all, I was busy burning the potatoes. At about that time, I remembered that I had followed the directions concerning placing a whole orange in the cavity of the first turkey, but it was only then that I recalled I was supposed to poke a couple of holes in the orange so the juices would escape. So, I grabbed a knife, opened the roaster lid, leaned into the bird and started to poke a hole in the orange. I'm sure you know what happened: a four-foot spray of juice from the orange shot out, thankfully missing me but hitting three cupboards, the whole left side of the counter, and a two-foot square area of floor. No more poking necessary.

It was during the orange ordeal that I also came upon the giblets packet I had not been able to find when I first washed turkey #1. Not wanting to embarrass myself further (as if this was even a possibility at this point), I quietly fished out the packet to throw it away (breaking it in half on the way, spilling its contents all over the counter, which provoked my sister-in-law to question all-too-loudly, "Hey, Laurie, whatcha got there?" Her Christmas present was immediately called into question).

At 4:00, I took the first turkey out of the roaster.

We ate at 5:15, only 105 minutes from the originally projected feeding frenzy. Not bad. It turned out that, after dinner, everyone decided to hang around and play ping-pong and talk about who in the family has created a living will, so by the time everyone was ready to head home, Turkey 2 was cooked, and we all got to hack off a slab of bird and have leftovers. Surprisingly, nobody took home any of the mashed potatoes.

Ever prepare for something, and have nothing turn out the way you planned? Thanksgiving was that for me, in every sense of the word. We ran out of toilet paper, we lost 11 ping-pong balls (I have no idea where they went, but I did find one in the cabinet under the bathroom sink the next day—don't ask), we nearly had to take a family trip to the ER, and we all ate so much food that we swore that none of us would need to eat for a week (this was before dessert—and most of the dessert was gone before the party was over).

It was one of the most fun memories I have of a family gathering. We talked, we laughed, we had way too many things go wrong.

It was perfect.

The Lord is continually using the lemons of our lives (or, in this case, oranges) to make juice for us to enjoy. How thankful I am to have a family that accepts the way I "cook," and who can laugh about nearly everything that happens along the way of life. How grateful I am that we could even get together as a family and not kill each other (this time).

How easy it was for me to see the face of Jesus on the faces of each person in that house (even the kid who kept hiding the ping-pong balls).

Perhaps you can see that God is, indeed, good, and He is doing a work in you today. Who knows? He may even use your goofy family to show you His wonderful work.

Pride
Heritage

My son began to share a German phrase that he learned from his buddy Joseph. It is that near-famous statement, "Hi, I am a giant squid."

They were in second grade.

Obviously.

So, after that conversation, Grandma started talking to my son about his nationalities, and how he has some German in his heritage, but he is quite a bit more Italian. Apparently, Ben had heard us talk about that before, because he carefully teaching-back the conversation with his grandma, explaining to her that he understood what she was trying to tell him, because he recognized that he himself is almost a full quarter Italian, but he's only a penny German.

You are German, you are Italian, you are Bulgarian, you are Haitian, you are French; we use the term "Christian" in the same way.

Can you make it incredibly obvious today that you are a believer in Jesus Christ, not only by your background, but by who you are in this moment? That's when the Lord can make a huge difference in you and the world.

After all, what matters is not being proud of where our families come from. What matters is being thankful to have a relationship with the Lord…wherever you're from.

PRIDE
I JUST CAN'T PLACE THE NAME

Three times in two days, I was confronted with people I should have known, but whose names escaped me. In one situation, I simply ignored the person until we were re-introduced by a mutual friend.

I'm quite mature.

In the second instance of not remembering a person's name, I tried to lie my way out, saying that her name isn't one that I remember easily, and she said that's understandable, since her name…is the same as mine: Laurie.

Great.

The third time happened while I was at a high school commencement service. It was at my own high school, only several years after my own graduation. A woman I had gone to high school with a couple of decades ago came up to me and started talking. I knew her, I really did, but her name simply escaped me. I tried to fake it, and I did fine…right up until she said, "You don't remember me, do you?" I tried to assure her that I did, and I started to talk about things we used to do together, playing basketball, and being in history class together, and actually going to school together from 6th grade through our senior year, but then she stopped me, and said, "Okay, then, what's my name?"

I was caught.

For the life of me, I couldn't remember. Finally, she told me, but by the time she got her last name out, I was about the size of a pea. I felt terrible.

I've decided that I'm just not going to go out in public anymore.

I long for others to feel special. I know that when I can't remember a person's name, they feel anything but special. Plus, it makes me look ridiculous—and maybe that's more important to me than I care to admit.

How grateful I am that God knows my name.

Jesus is the incarnate example of the word "offer." He offers us life, with no strings attached. All we have to do is accept what He offers: Himself. Are you offering yourself, or your money, or parts of your life, to the Lord or in the name of the Lord, with strings attached? That's not what He wants. He doesn't need your money. He doesn't need your help. He wants you to know Him, because He knows that's what you need.

PRIDE
MOTHER'S DAY

All of a sudden, at ages four and seven, my kids started to eat peanuts in the shell as their evening snack. Very quickly, they were both surprisingly good at separating the nut from the shell, and only every few minutes would I hear the *puh-puh-puh* sound of a shell being mistakenly put in a mouth.

So, there they were one Thursday evening, jammies on, shelling peanuts and having a great time, when I noticed out of the corner of my eye that Mary Jo, the four-year-old, wasn't moving. I turned to see her holding a perfect half of a peanut shell up to her ear. She was serious, sitting still, with her eyes squinted shut. I asked her, "Mare, what are you doing?"

She replied, "I'm trying to hear the ocean."

I asked, "What do you mean?"

She said, "You told me that if I put a shell to my ear, then I'd be able to hear the ocean."

I didn't have the heart to tell her that only happens if you put a *sea*shell to your ear. Besides, it seemed to her that she was doing just fine with the peanut shell.

I am so thankful to be a mom, but it's in moments like these that I realize how it's impossible to get parenthood right. And it's in moments like these that I am grateful that God's grace is big enough to fill the huge gaps that I leave. He is the perfect parent, knowing how to discipline me, how to teach me, and most of all, how to love me as His child.

Anything good that comes of them truly must come from Him. After all, I've got my kids putting peanut shells to their ears.

PRIDE
BE YOURSELF

Why is it that, under certain circumstances, we are willing to let go and simply be ourselves, when in other situations, with the same people, we feel the need to be something other than who we actually are? That, right there, is pride at its worst.

Take, for example, one Friday evening. It was my dad's birthday, so we went to the grandchildren's favorite burger joint.

Why we didn't go to my dad's favorite spot, I have no idea.

Seven adults, six children.

The adults were far outnumbered.

A good portion of dinner was spent in the adults trying to instruct the kids.

No, you may not put ketchup <u>there</u>.

No, I really don't think that you need to get up to use the restroom four times in one meal.

No, I'm quite sure that you don't need 13 quarters to play one video game.

And so on. The kids had a great time being kids, and the restaurant was so loud that nobody around seemed to notice that we might be the ones making all the noise. The adults, too, worked hard at being adults, sitting still, eating politely, trying to lead by example. *Here's what it looks like to be mature, kids. Follow what we do.*

Right up until the 8-month-old granddaughter, Brooke, wanted to show off her new-found talent: clapping.

I can only imagine what we must have looked like to those sitting around us, as the 13 of us started clapping in rhythm, trying like everything to get little Brooke to start clapping. Frankly, I think she was wise beyond her years, and was just trying to get us all to look ridiculous. And she succeeded. There we were, clap, clap, clapping, with those goofy, encouraging grins on all our faces, as we were working hard to get her to start clap, clap, clapping.

If there was no 8-month-old child looking on, would we *ever* consider sitting around a table in a crowded restaurant, clap, clap, clapping? And yet, that is who we are.

You are you. God has made you special, and His desire is for you to be the best you that you can be. Be who you are, all the time.

He expects nothing less.

PRIDE

THE GIFTED PROGRAM

Twice I have tried to make curtains for the goofy, really wide, not very long windows in one of the bedrooms in our house, and twice I have failed. So, yesterday I buckled: I decided to go to the home store and just buy some "plain vanilla" blinds.

I walked in and was immediately accosted by one of the employees. "Hi! How can I help you? What do you need? Where can I take you?"

I wasn't ready for that kind of assistance, and, quite frankly, it flustered me a bit. I regrouped in my head, tried to find magnetic north, and then I said, "Okay, I'm looking for…I'm looking for…" For the life of me, I could not remember the word "blinds." So I used my hands to try to describe what I was looking for.

So there we were, Tom the home store deputy and I, playing charades at the entrance of the home store as I tried to find the word "blinds" in my vocabulary. Once he understood that what I wanted had something to do with windows, he condescendingly guided me to the window treatment area. He quickly dumped me there, shaking his head as he walked away. "Great," I said barely audibly, "I've just set back women doing home projects about 20 years. What a dingbat. Clearly, I'm in the gifted program."

Right about that time, Bill, the Window Treatment Professional (at least that's what his nametag said), walked over. In a gentle voice, he asked me what I was looking for, what sort of material I wanted my blinds made from, how much I wanted to spend, and so on. After about 10 minutes and a lesson in blinds, he led me around the corner to exactly what I had had in my mind all along. He found the perfect size, handed the blinds to me, and turned to walk away.

I called out after him, "Bill, one more thing: am I going to be able to put these up myself?"

He stopped, turned around, smiled, and with a twinkle in his eye, he said, "Sure, you'll be able to put them up yourself. After all, you're in the gifted program, aren't you?"

I never intended for anybody to hear me ranting about being in "the gifted program." And right there, I was both humiliated because he had heard me say that, and thankful because saying those words had made it clear that I didn't have a clue what I was doing. He had heard me, even though I had no intention of anyone knowing how absolutely inept I am.

Now, God knows your thoughts even before you ever speak them. The reason you pray is not so that you can inform God of your heart, but so that you're tuned in to Him and what He has in store for you. That places you in the best Gifted Program ever.

PRIDE
GOWNS WIDE OPEN

In my hospital work, I spend quite a lot of time talking with patients and families about how to best take care of themselves emotionally and spiritually, and how to allow others to take care of them. I give suggestions for families that are coping with loss, such as: keep a pad of paper around and write down needs you have so that when people ask how they can help, you can read something off the list. I tell people, "Let your friends help you; it helps them feel needed, and it definitely helps you."

Then I had my second hip surgery in 6 weeks. I was laid up at home, and my husband arranged to have my mother come over and help.

I was mortified.

My mom decided she was going to catch us up on laundry--a tremendous offer, since I'd already been out of commission for awhile and, with 2 teenagers, laundry was stacking up. But all I could think of was the post-tornado-looking condition of the laundry room and that my dresser was not ready for inspection and shoes hadn't been put away and the spare room where I keep my clothes has become a dumping ground for all things with no home...and by the time she arrived, I was a mess, and it had nothing to do with the medications I was taking.

My pride had completely taken over my mind, and I couldn't bear to be vulnerable and let her take care of me...and see the monstrosity that was my house. I felt as if I was still wearing my hospital gown... and the tie straps had been cut off.

Most of us don't want to be vulnerable, but we do try to be humble (and pretend that our humility is vulnerability). Sometimes we think humility and vulnerability are synonymous, but they're not: humility is about not being too proud of your strengths, while being vulnerable is about admitting your weaknesses.

And it takes being vulnerable for others to actually care for you.

Interestingly, pride comes on the scene both when I'm not humble and when I'm not willing to be vulnerable.

> Psalm 10:4 states this: I*n his pride the wicked man does not seek The Lord; in all his thoughts there is no room for God.*

Pride makes us think we are good enough on our own and don't need God...or anyone else.

One verse I hear being quoted all the time is this one: "God won't ever give you more than you can handle."

Here's the problem with that: it's not in the Bible.

Anywhere.

That's because it's actually completely contrary to biblical teaching. Why? Because if I can handle it, then I don't need God.

We are regularly given situations we can't handle on our own. They teach us to recognize that we need The Lord every day.

I have no cause for being proud, and I have much cause to be vulnerable.

So where are you today? Are you searching the Bible to dispute what I just declared--that that verse isn't in there--or are you willing to let go and let others care for you in your need?

It's entirely up to you.

CHAPTER TWO: ENVY—IT'S NOTHING TO BE JEALOUS OF

ENVY
A MONSTER BY ANY OTHER NAME...

Luke 15:11-32, The Parable of the Lost Son

11Jesus continued: "There was a man who had two sons. 12The younger one said to his father, 'Father, give me my share of the estate.' So he divided his property between them.

13"Not long after that, the younger son got together all he had, set off for a distant country and there squandered his wealth in wild living. 14After he had spent everything, there was a severe famine in that whole country, and he began to be in need. 15So he went and hired himself out to a citizen of that country, who sent him to his fields to feed pigs. 16He longed to fill his stomach with the pods that the pigs were eating, but no one gave him anything.

17"When he came to his senses, he said, 'How many of my father's hired men have food to spare, and here I am starving to death! 18I will set out and go back to my father and say to him: Father, I have sinned against heaven and against you. 19I am no longer worthy to be called your son; make me like one of your hired men.' 20So he got up and went to his father.

"But while he was still a long way off, his father saw him and was filled with compassion for him; he ran to his son, threw his arms around him and kissed him.

21"The son said to him, 'Father, I have sinned against heaven and against you. I am no longer worthy to be called your son.'

22"But the father said to his servants, 'Quick! Bring the best robe and put it on him. Put a ring on his finger and sandals on his feet. 23Bring the fattened calf and kill it. Let's have a feast and celebrate. 24For this son of mine was dead and is alive again; he was lost and is found.' So they began to celebrate.

25"Meanwhile, the older son was in the field. When he came near the house, he heard music and dancing. 26So he called one of the servants and asked him what was going on. 27'Your brother has come,' he replied, 'and your father has killed the fattened calf because he has him back safe and sound.'

28"The older brother became angry and refused to go in. So his father went out and pleaded with him. 29But he answered his father, 'Look! All these years I've been slaving for you and never disobeyed your orders. Yet you never gave me even a young goat so I could celebrate with my friends. 30But when this son of yours who has squandered your property with prostitutes comes home, you kill the fattened calf for him!'

31" 'My son,' the father said, 'you are always with me, and everything I have is yours. 32But we had to celebrate and be glad, because this brother of yours was dead and is alive again; he was lost and is found.' "

Envy. Here's a reminder of the seven Deadlies: Pride, Envy, Gluttony, Lust, Anger, Greed, and Sloth. It's obvious from the last chapter that pride opens the door for the other Deadlies, because it's when we think we are better than others (or at least better than we really are) that the slide of pride takes us down to the pit of the other Deadlies.

And, while in personality envy is the closest Deadly Sin to pride, it is quite different from it—and the others—for this reason:

Envy is no fun at all.

Sure, sloth might not seem to be high on your list of must-haves, or anger either, or even gluttony, but let's face it: giving way to deep laziness can be fairly enticing at times, and releasing your frustration in a fit of rage can produce a little delight, and eating everything in sight with no control has its up-side, too.

Envy, however, is something entirely different. It is possibly the subtlest of the sins, and, therefore, the most insidious.

There is nothing good about envy.

In fact, one could probably tell a good deal about you if you were to disclose what it is you envy (if you ever were so brave). Envy comes in all sorts of packages; however, even though we might say that we typically envy some sort of thing, it's probably more accurate to say that it is the person who has the thing that becomes the true object of our envy.

Say, for example, that I see someone with something that I would like. I start to stew, because I can't have that thing. But my envy will not be directed toward that thing; it will hone in on the owner of the thing. *That person doesn't deserve it*, I might justify, *at least not as much as I do. Why can't I have that? How can I get it?* Or…*How can I get it from them?*

William Shakespeare came up with the perfect image when he wrote the following:

O, beware, my lord, of jealousy!
It is the green-eyed monster which doth mock
The meat it feeds on. (Othello, Act 3, Scene 3)

Ever feel yourself turning into that green-eyed monster, just like the Incredible Hulk or Jekyll and Hyde?

Maybe it's over somebody's shoes, or somebody's hair, or somebody's car, or somebody's life. But jealousy doesn't rear its green-eyed head just because we want something; it slithers in when we know that we can't have it…and somebody else does.

And often, I don't even realize that I want something until I see that other person with it. My life can be going along fine. I'm doing my thing, living as I should, pretty much content, and then *Wham!* That one over there—you know, the one from the last chapter who isn't as good as I am but in recognizing my pride I asked forgiveness about— yeah, that's the one—that person gets something, or has something they don't deserve…not like I deserve it.

There slides the knife in the heart.

What's more, people seem to be genuinely happy that the other person has that thing.

There shakes the salt in the wound.

All I want to do is stand up for what's right, for what's proper, for what's mine.

Uh…can anybody else see that lime-colored sludge creeping up behind me?

Whom do you identify with in the story of The Lost Son? Many of us with grown children can relate to the father, who watches in sadness as he stands by while his younger son makes poor choices. Then there are others of us with a checkered past who find a snug fit in the shoes of the prodigal himself.

Many of us in the church connect best with the older son. After all, we're the ones holding down the fort. We're the ones keeping track of the property, the people, and the paperwork. We're the ones who have been faithful. And yet, there goes Prodigal Pete, asking Dad for his share of the inheritance—and Dad's not even sick, much less dead.

Squanderer.

Down the road, we get news from a traveling salesman that he saw somebody that looked an awful lot like Pete in the next state, whooping it up and carrying on with all sorts of shady characters.

Loser.

Some time later, through the grapevine the family learns that the money's gone, and so is Pete; the most anyone knows is that Pete dragged himself in a drunken stupor to a farmer, but nobody has seen or heard from him since.

Can you imagine what was going through the older son's mind? *Got what he deserved, I guess. Time to get back to work. In the end, all is right with the world, and justice has been served. It's sad, sure, but fair is fair.*

And then one day, there's yelling outside the ranch back home. While the older son was working out in the field, he looked up: far off, he could see his father running away from the ranch, heading toward someone on the road. *Who is that guy? Is it...? No, it couldn't be.* And yet, the brother knew that walk anywhere. It was Pete, finally coming home with his tail between his legs.

Hmm. Guess I was wrong. Now we'll see true justice.

A little while later, though, back at the ranch, instead of seeing justice, the older brother heard something: music. As he got closer, he asked a servant what was going on. "Your brother has returned," he replied, "and your father has killed the fatted calf because he has him back safe and sound."

Huh?

Can you relate to the older brother's frustration? Can you identify with his anger? Can you see why he got so bent out of shape?

Then maybe this deadly sin is just for you.

Envy begins with pride—After all, I deserve better...at least better than you. Pride turns to envy when somebody already has that thing I need in order to prove that I'm better than you.

Read the story again. Track how you feel as you read it. Who knows? Maybe a green-eyed monster is lurking near you.

Maybe it's time to open the door, and shoo him out.

ENVY
ANGEL IN DISGUISE

These days, I work in a hospital system, overseeing several programs, from hospice to advance care planning to clinical ethics to our chaplains. I am in the perpetual presence of nurses, social workers, patients, and physicians.

Although I have spent years on the hospital floor, working directly with patients and participating in their care, I wish I was more medically savvy. I want to know how to perform procedures on patients and help them be cared for physically instead of just emotionally and spiritually.

[I figure you're thinking: "*Just* spiritually? That's the most important thing." And you'd be right. But I deal with the spiritual side every day, while those around me get to focus on things that are more black-and-white. Heart beating: you're alive. Heart stops: you die. There's something really intriguing about that...and not just because of all the cool toys like stethoscopes and such you get to use.]

Sure, there's the standing joke at my office that the clinicians are always willing to teach me how to place a catheter (I, however, am less willing), but other than being able to say STAT whenever I want my kids to get moving in the morning, I'm fairly useless in the medical category.

I know, I know—it's not my field. But I want it...at least in part because I can't have it and I'm surrounded by many who do have it.

Then there's this other weird thing: for some reason, friends and family seem to think that, because I work at a hospital, I am now qualified to give sound medical advice.

It makes no sense.

I had been working with the hospital for about a year when I got the call from my mom. She asked if I might be able to stop by their house in the next little while. When I asked why, she said that it was because "your father fell down and hit his head while he was at the jail today (it's not what you think...he was teaching G.E.D. classes there), and he's bleeding quite a lot. I think it should be looked at, so I thought maybe you could come and…look at it."

And do what: say, "Hey, he has a extracranial hemorrhage"? By the way, that means he has a head wound outside the skull.

Stat.

I told her to take him to the Emergency Department.

How helpful did she think I could be? Seriously. I have degrees in English Literature, French, Clinical Ethics, and Divinity (not the candy). Not in IV insertion, or vein splicing, or even checking blood pressure…and most definitely not in head trauma. I don't even trust myself to perform the CPR that I'm certified in.

So, like a good daughter, I drove over to my folks' house. And there's my dad, sitting at the table, the bleeding from his head-wound now stopped. I then did the smartest thing I could think of: I called one of the nurses. Like me, the nurse suggested that my dad head down to the ER, which he eventually did. And he's now fine. But the point is that even my parents thought that once I donned the title "hospital employee," that medical stuff would rub off on me.

Unfortunately for my family (and my patients), I've learned most of my medical jargon from Band-Aid commercials.

So, I admit it: I have some medical envy.

Couple that with what I actually do in my job, and it can be a recipe for disaster.

Take, for example, a trip I made to a nursing home one day. I was off to visit a hospice patient I had not seen before. As I was walking down the hall and around the corner toward the patient's room, one of the nurses at the nurses' station stopped me. She told me the demented patient I was about to see suffered by what she saw, and if she saw me walking in with dark-colored clothes, she would be scared. The nurse then stated that she did, however, have a solution: "Put on this white sheet (which she conveniently had next to her). Wrap it around yourself, and you'll look like an angel. She'll be really comforted."

So I did. I'm a rules follower, after all, and this was someone medical telling little ol' me what to do. You bet I'm going to listen.

I wrapped myself up in the sheet and headed to the entrance once again. "Oh, wait," the nurse called out. "I forgot to tell you one more thing. If you flap your arms up and down, she really will think you're an angel, and she'll feel lots better."

So I turned around and headed into the patient's room, all the while flapping my now-flowing and now-white arms.

Let me just say this: the patient was comforted. Without breaking any HIPAA laws, I can tell you that we had a delightful, peace-centered conversation. And when I left the patient—still flapping my arms—and headed out the door toward the nurses' station, I was greeted with a whole gaggle of nurses, and every one of them was trying to keep from snorting in laughter.

Apparently, Nurse Ratched was kidding about the "flapping the wings" stuff. She took back the sheet, practically crying with laughter, and thanked me for making the afternoon worth it.

I told her, "You're welcome," and headed out. But all I could think about was how embarrassed I was that I had fallen for the "flap your arms like an angel" trick. Moreover, I was envious: I'm usually the one in the position to make people do funny things (because people listen to the director, I can tell them to do almost any goofy thing…AND THEY DO IT). I wanted to be over there with the group of nurses, where the grass was greener. I wanted to be part of the cool gang that got people to do silly things. Nobody wants to be in the hot seat; we all want to be in the know, on the inside, jiggy with the situation.

A few months later, we had a new nurse join the hospice team. For the first couple of days, she was really quiet, particularly around me. Then, finally she spoke. One of the first things she said was something directed to me: "I was that nurse at the nursing home that made you flap your arms like an angel. You made my day. Thanks."

All of a sudden, she was on my turf. I hadn't remembered she was that nurse. She never would have had to say anything.

But she did.

And she made me part of the group—that "in" crowd.

I was surprised how much her gesture humbled me. Through one comment, Sandy helped me feel included.

And all of a sudden, I wasn't envious. I didn't feel desperate. I didn't feel like I was on the outside. I didn't feel like the last third-grader picked for the kickball team.

Because she made me feel part of the team.

Now, go back to the Gospel story of the two brothers. The older brother was a rules follower. He did what he was supposed to. And he figured that he'd get his just reward in the end: he'd get the good life, and his brother would not. So he stayed home, he kept doing what was required of him, and he missed out on a whole heap of trauma…all the while staying in his father's good graces (because, in the end, that's what this is about, isn't it—it's about being well-loved by the father). But when the younger brother came home and <u>was welcomed with his father's open arms,</u> the older brother was steaming.

Wait—wait a minute—this isn't how it's supposed to be. By taking his inheritance while Dad is still alive, Junior essentially says to the world that Dad is dead. Then he blows his cash on fast cars and fast women. He doesn't call, he doesn't write, we don't know if he's alive or dead. Meanwhile, I stay home and do all the chores—mine and his. I'm home every night for the family dinner. I never miss curfew. I'm doing everything I'm supposed to, and Junior does nothing. And which one of us gets the big, fat party? Doesn't anybody besides me see what's going on here?!

There's a reason many of us in the church can relate to the older brother. We feel like we're doing what we're supposed to be doing. We faithfully attend worship every Sunday. We participate in church cleanup days. We bring food to the potlucks. We teach Sunday school long after our own kids have left the nest. We cut checks for exactly 10% of our gross income, even if it means that we'll be making sacrifices throughout the next month. Because that's what we're supposed to do.

Then, all of a sudden, a familiar couple enters the church. These are the two that teased everybody in high school in order to look good themselves. They didn't care who they walked on, because they were the beautiful people. They lived fast and hard with Daddy's money. Later, you had heard that, somewhere along the way, the beautiful houses and the beautiful cars and the beautiful lifestyle were all taken away.

They'd squandered everything they'd gotten.

And in your mind, you shrugged and thought, *Well, at least somebody finally got what they deserve.*

But now they're here. And nobody's shunning them. Instead, people are greeting them, and welcoming them, and already playing the "remember when you caught the winning pass in that game" game.

And in your mind, all you can think is: *Wait—wait a minute—this isn't how it's supposed to be. Doesn't anybody besides me see what's going on here?!*

We want justice. We want to know that the world makes sense. After all, if I knew that I could whoop it up and party all the time and have no consequences, then why would I choose to follow the rules? My demand for justice sometimes actually stems from deep-rooted envy.

They're not getting what they deserve.

Here's the rub in all of this—and if may be painful to hear.

Life is not about getting what we deserve.

You may be sitting in your living room, thinking about all that you've done for the church, and wondering why those vagabonds over there (who never commit, or at least don't follow through if they do commit) are getting special treatment. But remember, we don't do things in order to earn something. As followers of the Lord, we are to live in a way that's pleasing to God...out of thanks for what He's already done for us. And if someone has walked away from a relationship with Christ, then we should be like the father, ready to welcome him back and celebrate when he gets here.

Because, while it's easy to forget our own sins and remember everybody else's, we need to recall that we have been given as much grace as the next person—more than we'll ever need.

And I know I need a lot.

The father does it right: he talks with the older son and brings him back into the fold. He makes the older son a co-conspirator in the game of grace. He gives the family an opportunity to be a family again.

With a little perspective shift, it's possible to get completely away from envy. When I recognize how much grace I've been given, then I don't have to be keeping track of how it lines up with anybody else's grace. Instead, I can just live and realize: I already am part of the "in" crowd.

I hope you are able to live envy-free today.

ENVY
HANDS IN POCKETS

We all know there are two kinds of stores. There are kid-friendly stores, and there are hands-in-pockets stores. You know the hands-in-pocket stores: the ones with blown glass and fine china. The other ones—the ones with remote-control cars you can try out, or ball pits you can jump into—those are kid-friendly.

For the most part, adults, by the time they become adults, know the difference. But kids are a different story. Something shiny in a store filled with glass cases is not an invitation to touch. And yet, those are the very stores kids seem attracted to.

My daughter, at age seven, asked me to take her to the mall to look at necklaces. So we headed to the only mall in our town, and I began to walk toward one of those dollar store stores. But when I got to the shop entrance, I realized that Mary Jo was no longer beside me. She was next door…at a "real" jewelry store, drooling over the "shiny" gold and diamond necklaces under the glass cases. They were "much prettier than the ones at the kid store." But, try as she might, she couldn't get her hands to the jewelry, because the glass was in the way. And touching the glass left fingerprints behind, which didn't exactly make the well-dressed but stern jewelry lady very happy.

This was definitely a hands-in-pockets store.

I walked over to give my daughter a joking reprimand—after all, this was not the sort of jewelry a child needed. It was beyond her. *After all, this one is a hands-in-pockets store, Mary Jo.* But when I arrived next to her and looked down and saw what she was staring at, I couldn't take my eyes off of it, either. It was stunning. It was shiny.

If only I could touch it.

But I couldn't touch it…not even with a ten-foot wallet. And that just bugged me.

We don't envy things we know we can have. If the reason I don't have something is because I have made another choice, then I probably won't be envious, because I could choose differently, if I wanted to. But if I feel like my hands are tied, and someone else has what I want, or someone else is what I want to be, then that green-eyed monster starts creeping up behind me once again, convincing me to cry out those familiar words:

That's not fair!

If this is you, then it has probably come time to ask yourself a question: Is that what you really want: for life to be fair? Are you sure you want what you deserve? Be careful before you declare too boldly what it is you think you want; after all, you just might get it.

As an adult, do you feel like your life is still being run by the Hands-In-Pockets rule that is a cloud covering your heart and hindering your hope?

Don't Touch.

Do you see a car that you like, but somewhere deep inside, something is telling you, "You can't have it," and it only makes you want it more?

Don't Touch.

Maybe you are sitting next to someone who is eating something that you would like, but "That's not for you" fills your brain.

Don't Touch.

Is a friend going on a vacation that you would love to take, but there's a brick wall blocking the way between your desire and the travel agent?

Don't Touch.

Did the fellow teacher next door just receive great accolades, while you, after decades of hard work and commitment and creativity, haven't received anything other than every disease that those rotten kids have brought in each cold and flu season?

Don't Touch.

And finally, you just want to cry out: *Why not?!?!*

Envy. It's about wanting something you don't have, but someone else does, and your blood is reaching boiling point because you think you deserve it.

The older brother in Luke 15 was envious. He had always been faithful. So faithful. He never left his dad's side, and he never squandered the inheritance (or even asked for it before his time). Meanwhile, the younger son got the fatted calf, he received a gold ring, he was clothed with a cloak and even thrown a giant party.

How long have you been the eldest son?

How many years have you been so committed, and disciplined, and willing, but you've never been thrown the party, and, in fact, you've been directed, *Don't Touch*?

Being a Christian isn't easy. That's because it's not about accolades, or gold rings, or beautiful cloaks, or lavish banquets. It's about knowing that you are in the loving arms of a Father who is thankful that you've remained faithful.

In your heart, you have an opportunity. Instead of crying out, *Why Not?*, you get to cry out, *Not my will, but Yours be done.*

I know, I know, it's easier said than done.

But try it. In a day or even a moment of envy, try redirecting your thoughts up instead of out: *God, have mercy on me, a sinner. Help me to love you, and to know and feel like that is enough, and that I don't need to touch.*

I just need to follow You.

Envy

The Book Deal

A while back, I entered a little essay contest. It was just me…and about 4,999 other entrants. The challenge was to write about when you first realized that you had become an adult.

First, I wrote the piece. It was a funny take on my relationship with my mom: recognizing that I had actually become the mother that I have spent a lifetime mocking my own mom for being. It went from my head to paper easily, but when I finished, I wasn't sure it was worth sending in (mostly because I was a little afraid that my mom wouldn't like it, since she despises being made the center of attention, and, surprisingly, she doesn't like to be mocked. She's a little weird that way). So I emailed it to my folks, and then I actually forgot about it.

A few days later, my parents came to dinner. While we were sitting on the porch with my mom and me chatting away, my dad chimed in, telling me that he laughed harder that morning than he's laughed in a long time. I was shocked when he told me what made him laugh so much: that essay. My mom even admitted that she thought it was amusing.

I decided that was confirmation to me. I got the essay back out, edited it, and then sent it off to a friend to take a slightly more objective look at it. Since she's a reader of the magazine that was sponsoring the essay (and she really likes to critique things), she was excited to take part in my entry.

That's when the first stumbling block came along. It hadn't crossed my mind to consider whether I actually wanted criticism, constructive or otherwise. I didn't. I wanted her to say that it was the best and funniest thing she's read in a long time. I wanted her to tell me she had to grab the kitchen towel off the counter to wipe the tears of laughter streaming from her face. I ached for her to tell me she had immediately walked to the neighbor's house (people she doesn't know, by the way) just to show off this essay that would soon be deemed a literary masterpiece.

She didn't.

Instead, she went to the computer to do some research. Instead of sending me confirmation of my genius, she came back at me with information. She said that last year's winner went the sentimental route. She said that's what the judges of these sorts of essays seem to go for. Sure, she said, my essay is funny (*Funny? Just how funny? Fall-on-the-floor funny, or inside-I'm-laughing-you-just-can't-tell-from-the-serious-look-on-my-face-because-I'm-busy-researching-why-this-essay-isn't-going-to-win funny?*). But I would probably be better off heading down that same sentimental road that seemed to work in the past.

My first response was: *You don't know what you're talking about. You're no writer. I'm the writer. I mean, I'm not an official writer, but I have made money with my writing (four hundred dollars for a joke I submitted to Reader's Digest in the year 2000, thank you very much).*

My second response was: *I'm going to convince you (my girlfriend, that is) that this essay is going to win.* I edited it again. I made it even funnier. I twisted her arm and beat her will until she caved and told me that it was the best thing she'd ever read and they'd be fools not to give me the grand prize.

That's more like it.

So I submitted my entry, and I waited.

Six months.

For the last month, I checked the magazine's website nearly every day on the off-chance that they might come to a decision early—after all, surely after they had read my essay, the rest would be placed in the "good but not quite good enough" pile.

And then the day finally came (and not early, I might add). The winner was announced.

It was some English professor from Arizona, or New Mexico, or one of those states that wasn't mine.

And guess what? Her essay was wonderful. It was well-written. It was sentimental.

Not that I read it right away. I nearly cancelled my subscription to the magazine, because I figured that if they had such poor taste in essay contest entries, maybe they didn't actually know how to do the other things they claim to have wisdom in, like taking red wine stains off of a light-colored carpet or being able to provide the perfect tools for organizing my garage. I was ready to boycott this publication altogether, so I went online to their website. I found the page that had information about the essay contest, including a place where people could make personal comments.

I was stunned by the things others wrote about the essay contest.

Dozens of people had written in on the first day. *It wasn't fair—the winner was a professional,* one person argued. The next one agreed: *She's an English professor, which is practically like getting an insider to win the contest.* The other comments were like that, too—bashing the contest and the winner because it simply wasn't a fair fight.

I admit it—at first I agreed.

Yeah! This chick knows the English language better than the rest of us, so of course she shouldn't be allowed to enter the contest.

Yeah! A professor is a professional, and professionals shouldn't be allowed to enter a contest geared toward, uh, non-professionals.

Yeah!

That's when I realized I had fallen victim to the sin of envy. I, too, was searching for any essay contest loophole so that I could slip right in. I wanted to win, and I didn't want her to win. So I was going to beat down her essay, or her qualifications, or the contest itself in order to prove that the essay was rigged, because that must be the only reason why I didn't win.

Then I read her essay. It was worthy of winning.

My envy nearly caused me to cancel my subscription to a magazine I love, and it nearly got me involved in a complaining frenzy the likes of which hasn't been seen in these parts since Neighbor Johnson built his fence three inches over his property line onto the Rasmussen property.

But that's another story.

ENVY

LOOKING FOR LOVE

Jealousy is all the fun you think they had.

Erica Jong, in "Fear of Flying," wrote these words.

How true is that?!

Envy is the great distorter; it skews our view of ourselves and others. It makes us want what we don't have, and want what we think others do have. It makes us choose poorly…and waste way too much of our lives and ourselves.

You know, most people don't know what "prodigal" really is. They think it means "lost." But the word "prodigal" means "excessively wasteful."

Makes sense, especially in the story of the Prodigal Son.

The younger son already had the perfect love. That's obvious when this frivolous son demanded his inheritance…and the dad said yes. He was already in the perfect relationship at home. But he thought he saw green grass…over there. So he took his toys and left to find something better, because surely he deserved it.

What he found was that he left the best thing he could hope for: real love.

That love wasn't to be found in money. It wasn't to be found in parties. It couldn't be had by going away.

That love was found in the arms of his father.

And envy almost destroyed it forever.

Why do we look all over the house and under the couch and between cushions for love, when we are already being offered true and perfect love, and it's standing right in front of us? Why do we think our lives aren't enough, that there is something better, something exciting, something, well, more?

Because we let envy take over instead of letting Jesus take over.

Josh Billings wrote:

Love looks through a telescope; envy, through a microscope.

Today, try to avoid looking for love in all the wrong places. If you want, spend some time in a quiet place or at home on your knees. Or sit at your desk, and quietly bow your head, and tell the Lord what's going on and what you're looking for. Jesus is there, you know.

You don't have to go far, if you're looking for love.

ENVY
I WANNA PLAY

Want to see raw envy? Go sit on some bleachers. That guy who is yelling at the ref or screaming at the coach, thinking he could certainly do better and would surely lead the team to victory--often, that guy is the one trying to work out his (or her) envy. But he lacks the time it takes, the commitment, or the control to coach the big-leaguers (or the Little Leaguers). So, he must resign himself to marinating in envy. And that envy comes out in judgment, back-biting, and gossip.

Envy is "intent on the destruction of the happiness of others," wrote Immanuel Kant. Taking away others' happiness is a key to envy, since the envious tend to be collectors of injustice.

It is time to live the life that Jesus died for.

Easier said than done these days.

Even when we're not feeling envy ourselves, sometimes we get lost in the lives of others as they live in envy. Television programs, movies, songs—they all speak of an emotion that we understand all-too-well: that song-and-dance with Big, Green, Ugly himself.

Have you ever seen the television show "Survivor"? One early premiere episode had the 20 contestants rowing in their pontoon boat—they were told that the beach where they would be living was one mile beyond them. On the beach were two immunity necklaces: one for the first man to reach the beach, and one for the first woman (the wearer of the immunity necklace would not be voted off the island that week). The thing that the group had to decide was the best way to get to the beach.

At first, they all got into the pontoon boat and began to paddle—let's face it, a mile swim is a pretty long distance. They began by working together. But pretty soon, players started to jockey for position in the front. A few of the girls left their paddles and shuffled up toward the bow of the boat, so that when others decided to dive in, they'd be in perfect position.

How do you think the other contestants—the ones still paddling—felt? It was all caught on tape.

Then, with probably about a ½ mile to go, one woman decided it was time. She said she was a pretty good swimmer, and, more importantly, she didn't want any of the others to have immunity, so she took a fabulous-looking swan dive off the bow and into the beautiful, blue water. Almost immediately, one of the young, buff men did the same.

Now, those women who were sitting at the front of the boat had to sort of scoot out of the way so that these two could dive off. And for a split-second after the two disappeared in the water, you could see back on top of the water that there was some consternation over whether others should do this, too; after all, they weren't just going to sit around while somebody else was getting the necklace that was clearly made just for them! But then, something happened: from the moment the man and the woman in the water came up for air and started swimming, it was clear that they had made a poor choice: the boat overtook them immediately, and they were left behind. In the end, the first two in the water were the last two to get out of the water…by a long shot.

You can imagine how envious they were of the others who waited patiently in the boat. You can also imagine how upset the rowers were by the end, when they were tired and the ones who just sat and waited had plenty of energy to swim the last hundred yards to the beach.

So, in this game of life, where are you finding yourself today:

On the sidelines, complaining about the ref?

In the game, complaining about the players?

Or heading out to participate fully, enjoying every moment of it?

The choice is yours.

Envy
A Form of Flattery

My mom, my daughter, and I love "Anne of Green Gables." Lucy Montgomery writes the story (which was later made into a movie) of a little orphan girl who comes to live with an old couple on Prince Edward Island in eastern Canada. The stories that follow her arrival describe Anne Shirley's life as she grows up, sees the world, and finds herself realizing that the life she always dreamed of living can be found in the very place she tried so hard to escape: home.

In one scene, Anne was a young teacher preparing for a benefit ball. Surrounded by the students she was charged to be dorm mother for, Anne finished getting herself ready, then asked her charges, "Well, what do you think?"

One of the girls replied, "Oh, Miss Shirley, I'm going to wear my hair just like that when I turn 18."

Anne turned away from the mirror and faced the girls. "You darlings. Imitation is the sincerest form of flattery."

It's true. Imitation is the sincerest form of flattery. It means that someone respects your judgment, your taste, your sense of style, or your wisdom enough to want to imitate—to be like—you.

But the line between flattery and jealousy is a thin one, indeed. Once imitation turns to emulation—the desire to be as good as or better than another—well, then there's trouble. Big trouble. Because the struggle then is not with having something in particular, or looking some way that will make you feel good, but in having something that makes you look better than another person.

Have you ever complimented someone on something—maybe it was their work, maybe it was their outfit, maybe it was their children—but all the while, the words that came out of your mouth didn't quite fit the words that were swimming around in your brain? While you were going on and on about those delightful children, your brain was going on and on about how unruly they were in Sunday school, and how you would just love to see how those little nightmares—er, I mean angels—turn out in about fifteen years. Then we'll see how delightful they really are!

Sometimes we do all the right things, and we say all the right words, but we're wrong. That's because our hearts are in the wrong place. False flattery is no flattery at all. Working for God with a heart that is grumpy is of no good use at all, either.

Remember: our job as Christians, as children of God, as humans, really, is to lift up the Lord, not ourselves. The moment I start worrying about myself is the moment the trouble begins.

Socrates wrote: "Envy is the ulcer of the soul." Today, you have an opportunity to relieve that ulcer, maybe before it ever begins. Treat it with 2 tablets of true and sincere kindness, and call on Him.

ENVY

HAIR TRAUMA

So, the church service is over. Sermon's done, music's been sung, offering's been taken, and now they're filing out the back. And there I am, the preacher, standing at the doors to the sanctuary, ready to greet the parishioners as they head out to apply every drop of wisdom that I have labored over presenting to them in the previous 59 ½ minutes.

On this particular Sunday, four of the elderly church matriarchs encircle me. One woman--let's call her Eunice—has been designated their speaker. "We just wanted to tell you that we were listening intently," Eunice begins. And I'm feeling pretty good so far. But then she continues. "And together, after discussing it throughout the service, we agreed that we really liked your hair...three weeks ago."

And then they broke the circle and walked in a single-file line out the sanctuary door and toward the coffee table.

Nothing about the Scripture passage. Nothing about the message. Nothing about what the Lord is doing.

That 30 minutes after the service is the bane of my existence. It's always felt odd for me. After all, at what other job do you work for an hour (so church members think), then head to the back of the office for people to shake your hand and tell you what a wonderful job you did?!

Other pastors tell me it's their favorite time, because people come to greet them and shake their hand and tell them what a delightful service it was. The pastors get lots of information regarding their parishioners, what's going on in the life of the church, and what's going on in the community.

I get frequent comments about my hair. And my clothes. And my shoes. And my teeth.

The grass looks an awful lot greener down the street at the Baptist church.

The hair comment hit close to home for me, because my hair has always been a source of personal trauma. In the eighth grade, I had a permanent that went awry, and my brothers started calling me Wig. My middle brother still calls me Wig.

It's been thirty-plus years.

Getting a haircut has always involved drama as well. I have taken to carrying Kleenex (okay, I admit, and a brush, hair gel, hair spray, and a scarf), in my car so that, after my haircut, I can sneak to my car, cry my eyes out, redo my do, and get my face dry by the time I return to work or home. It appears that no amount of describing, explaining, instructing, or even whining will result in my getting the haircut that I really want.

But finally, I think I am coming to an understanding of why I struggle so much with getting my hair cut: because my hairdresser and I have never understood who is in charge.

I keep going to these salons that have names that are supposed to instill confidence in me, the consumer. Trendsetters, Hair Fantasy, Signatures, Beauty Secrets, Classy Cuts (I want a classy cut), Fantastic Sam's, Super Cuts, Great Clips—the titles alone should make me feel good about walking in, knowing that I'm going to walk out feeling great. And yet, every time, I'm reaching for the tissue box. My favorites are the salons with the name "Master" in them. Master. Obviously, they know what they are doing.

Some of these salons require an appointment two months in advance—how in the world am I supposed to know when I'm going to have hair trauma and need a good cry? The fact is, with all the titles, with all the experience (and I'm not knocking the hair salons themselves), they must not be the problem.

The problem is with me—I have never realized who's really in charge.

Me.

The hairdresser is providing a service—for me.

Why does that sound revolutionary to me?

Now that I've discovered (unfortunately after my most recent haircut) that I am the one who is in charge, I'm getting rid of the tissue in my car. Once I put that relationship in the right perspective, I realize I have all the freedom in the world to ask for what I want, and to expect that what I ask for is what I will receive. The hairdresser, too, has more freedom, because that person will have some guidelines within which to work. For my hairdresser, freedom is not doing whatever she wants and then watching me as I run out the door, hide behind the lamppost, duck behind a parked car, then run like the wind to my car. Freedom is knowing what I am looking for in a style, and then being able to creatively get there so I am satisfied.

It's all about knowing and understanding the relationship.

And it's the same principle that I get to apply to the freedom I have, when I recognize that I am not the Master; Jesus is.

My body, for example, is the house. But I am not the owner of the house—although I often get confused into thinking that I am. No, instead, I am the contractor, the one who has been given instructions on how to build, and strengthen, and decorate this house for the owner to live in it. That owner, that Master…is the Lord. When I know my place, and know who I am, and who I am not, then I can see why Paul writes to the Corinthian church, "You are God's temple." It makes more sense, when I realize that I don't own this house; I'm just renting it while I build it for the Master to reside in it…in me.

Envy takes over when I think I'm in control of the plantation…and I wish I had somebody else's field. Erma Bombeck put it wonderfully: "The grass is always greener over the septic tank."

I just have to remember what's under the green grass, because it's not always better than what I already have.

After all, I have more than I need.

ENVY

YOGURT ENVY

I was 18 years old and on my first airplane trip alone. Between New Jersey and back home to Washington State, there was a four-hour layover in Chicago. It was crowded, it was fast-paced, it was confusing...

It was great. I decided I was born for this.

Even so, I didn't know what I was supposed to do. I felt like, well, like an 18-year-old from little ol' Yakima, Washington, on her first trip to the big city; in other words, I felt out of place. I wanted to be comfortable, because I felt like this was what I was made for: city life. But I had no idea how I was supposed to act in order to really look the part.

As I sat in my seat at my gate, wondering what I would do for the next 3 hours and 45 minutes, I noticed a woman walking by. She had an air of confidence. Her carry-on bag was slung over her shoulder, and she walked as if she knew what was around the next corner of her life. In her left hand, she held a Styrofoam container of peach-colored frozen yogurt. In her right hand, she held the spoon. I watched as this woman took a spoonful of yogurt, lifted it up, and twisted the spoon before she took a bite, so that the frozen yogurt was upside-down once it reached her mouth. She did that time and time again—not too hurriedly, but not too slowly or deliberately, either—as she walked down the crazy corridor. She seemed completely unaffected by the thousands of people who crossed her path on her way to wherever.

I immediately got up and went in search of the frozen yogurt stand. If I can get that same yogurt, then maybe I, too, can be as confident, as comfortable, as grown-up as that woman.

I spent the next couple of hours looking for an ice-cream stand. All I found were fourteen restrooms and a shoe-shiner.

I've been searching for that dish of frozen yogurt ever since.

Oh, if I could only have what she has, then I'll be happy, I've thought to myself.

Sounds sort of silly, doesn't it? Or, does it hit closer to home than you really want to admit?

The younger son, the wasteful son of Luke 15, was looking for the ultimate frozen yogurt of his day. Actually, the older son was looking for it, too. He just figured it came in a different package.

You know, life can be fine when you think that A plus B equals C.

A: I work hard.
B: I obey my father.
C: I get my just reward.

That was the mentality of the older son. I'm going to stay here. I'm going to do what my father says. In the end, I'll get praise and glory.

Can you imagine how the older son must have felt as he was working? He's plowing along, and then he stops.

What's that sound? Do I hear...a party going on? Wait a minute, I'm out in the field!

One element of envy comes in feeling like we're being left out of the party. If we're honest, we'll hope that the party is actually for us. Cake, presents, music, more presents...because, after all, I deserve it. Short of that, though, I at least want to be on the guest list. But then to know that there's a party, it's not for me, and they started without me—ooh, that's brutal. What's more, Dad's throwing the party for my brother?!

You have got to be kidding.

He hasn't spent his life doing what's right. In fact, when he left, I had to keep working my own chores, plus take over his. I want justice! I want what's coming to me!

More than anything, I don't want him to have my frozen yogurt.

Is Dad saying that now I can go squander his money, live the wild life, and return, and he'll have a party for me? Maybe I should—maybe it'll be the only way I'll get to have a party at all!

But now, just think about how a slight turn in perception and perspective can make such a difference. Imagine that the older son came to his senses and continued the conversation in his head with these words:

Wait a minute. Maybe by living a life that I know is where I'm supposed to be…maybe that is the better party. I know I'm loved, and I don't have to go to another country to see how good life is. I know I am being groomed for the family business, and, sure, it's not as exciting as some people's jobs, but it has purpose, and I have purpose. Yeah, and okay, I suppose it's good to welcome my bro back. It's been hard to play ping-pong alone (isn't that what all brothers do together?). I guess he's been living in a world with no net below him, while I have all kinds of security, because I know what it is to spend every day with my father.

The younger brother simply forgot how important that time with the father was. The younger brother was the one that sinned originally… but the older brother began to sin in his envy. Righteousness can become self-righteous with the flick of a switch.

Envy can be defused, and pretty easily, in fact. As the policemen at a crime scene say: "Show's over, step aside, folks, nothing to see here, move along." Change what it is you're looking at. Instead of looking to the thing that piques your curiosity (and dangerous scenes, crime scenes, car wrecks, and situations of sin pique our curiosity like nothing else), look to the One who really matters: the Lord. Jesus is the remedy for Envy.

He is a cool drink of water over a hard and crusty heart. He's the cup of frozen yogurt to one who is ready to fit into His plan, and not my prodigal plan. Seek Him today, and you'll find Him. And instead of living with a green-eyed monster, you just might find that the grass that is greener is in your very own yard.

ENVY

PRISON PARTICIPATION

Do you ever feel like you want to be part of everything just so you don't miss out on anything?

Me, too. What's more, if I <u>know</u> that something great is happening, and I can't be part of it, oh, that makes my ears start to burn.

Let me give an example of what I'm talking about.

For a season, I counseled a couple in pre-marital counseling. I've done this for many couples preparing to marry. But this situation was slightly different: the groom was housed in a maximum security prison.

Two of us drove across the mountains to the prison, where I counseled the woman, and the other person counseled the man. On one particular visit, the bride-to-be had to leave early for work. So, I walked out of the cafeteria, past the ultraviolet screener, through the three electronic firewall doors, past the scanner, down the steps, around the front desk, and out the door. I stayed with her a little while, then I got into my car, which was right under the tower where the security guard with his rifle pointed in my direction spent the next hour watching me make phone calls and enjoy a little nap.

I was to return to the other counselor and the inmate an hour later, but when the time came and I re-entered the building and showed my ID to the guard at the front desk, he said I couldn't enter; I had already been there once, and they don't allow re-entry in a single day. Besides, there was only one more hour left of visiting time anyway.

In no time, I had convinced myself that something great was going on in there. I was sure the other counselor and the inmate were having a great conversation—because that's what happens when I'm not around.

Seething with envy, I stewed by the entrance. The guard told me I was welcome to wait outside in the beautiful sunshine if I wanted (already did that), or to walk around a bit (already did that), just as long as I didn't wait in my car (already did that). So, I walked back outside and sat on a concrete picnic bench, spending the next 20 minutes watching the odd-looking bug on the picnic table try to eat my arm for a mid-afternoon snack.

Finally, I just got bored. So, I walked back up the big steps and sat on the bench where I watched those desperate for fresh air come out for a cigarette. As I sat there, and stared at the big clock that said 4:00 p.m. (only 30 minutes left of visiting hours—hooray!), all of a sudden, I realized something—something I hadn't recognized for the past couple of hours as I was having my pity-party: I was getting exactly what I had been praying for for weeks, no, maybe months: a break. I was getting an afternoon "off," and here I was, being a little pill about the whole thing. So, right there, I started to pray. Immediately, I realized that my anxiety had come because I wanted to be in the middle of the action, but I hadn't paid attention to the fact that I was in the middle of the action—God's action.

So there I was, sitting, smiling, and talking to God, when a man came out and sat across from me. Had he come out just five minutes before, he would have gotten an entirely different Laurie. But now, as he sat down and looked over at me and commented on the beautiful, warm day, he saw a person who was thankful to be there. And, though I was curious about his story (he didn't look like a typical inmate visitor, and he was wearing a button-down shirt that had "Champions for Life" embroidered on it), I smiled and waited for him to begin talking, which he soon did.

He runs a ministry, this man named Dennis, based out of Texas: Champions for Life. Their core team flies around the country to prisons, then gets about 200 volunteers from the area to infiltrate the prison for a weekend. Celebrities, football players, and strong-men come out and put on a show—tearing phone books in two, bending lead pipes, breaking baseball bats with their knees—in order to attract the inmates in the yard. Then, one-by-one, the volunteers talk with the inmates about Jesus. He said this work is so much easier than going door-to-door sharing the gospel, because people in their homes are comfortable, and they have control over their lives; they don't need a God to help them. But here, the prisoners know what consequences are all about. They have no control over anything in their lives. They are much more open to hearing about The Lord.

It didn't take me long to realize that Dennis was as curious about what I was doing there as I was about him; I took it as a compliment that he thought I looked like I didn't really belong outside a prison, either.

After a little surface banter, he asked if I perhaps recognized him. I thought, *Should I?* Surely he wasn't from Yakima, and I wasn't sure where I could possibly know him.

He asked if I knew about Charles Manson and the book, *Helter Skelter*. Uh, yeah. Of course.

Turns out that this man standing across from me was one of Charles Manson's best friends. When "Charlie," as this man called him, was placed in prison, this buddy tried to break him out of prison. He then spent seven years behind bars himself. While incarcerated, this man's children lived with the Manson family.

And then he came to know the Lord.

This man looked like he belonged behind a desk, not behind bars. He could pass for an executive, not an inmate.

"It's a testament to what the Lord can do, if you let Him," he said.

And now he brings that testament to other men in prison.

What a gift I received that day. Turns out I didn't miss out on anything. Instead, I was part of something most exciting, and the action was where I was. That other counselor, the one in with the inmate? When he heard about my experience, well, let's just say that green is not his color. He proved it.

The action is wherever you are, too. In fact, He's probably right under your nose. You might miss Him, if you start looking too far ahead and not right in the spot He has placed you.

I nearly did.

ENVY

DOCTOR, DOCTOR

I work in a hospital. Every person--from the person who washes the walls on down to the CEO himself--every person learns to end every conversation, whether it's with a patient or a coworker, with this question: *Is there anything else I can do for you?*

That question has opened the door to numerous unexpected conversations and activities.

Recently, I was meeting with a physician and a social worker at our hospice house, which is about 3 miles from the hospital. We reached the end of the meeting, and, I admit that it was more out of habit than intention when I asked, "Is there anything else I can do for you?" The doctor, with a wink in his eye that I didn't notice, stated that he had left his stethoscope on the fifth floor of the hospital, and if I might go get it and drive it back to his office before clinic started, it would be really helpful to him.

I was the one that offered, so off I went (leaving behind a stunned doctor--something that is very, very rare; he was shocked I would comply). I drove back to the hospital, parked, zipped up to the fifth floor, found the stethoscope immediately, and began to make the trek back to the car.

Except that something happened along the way.

I should tell you that I'm fairly well-known in most departments of our hospital...except the fifth floor, because it's the floor where patients go post-surgery and are often in and out quite quickly and don't deal much with my area. Also, as a woman, I wear women's clothing (obviously), and apparently women's clothing designers figure that women don't need pockets. You can imagine the scene: I held my keys in one hand as I headed from the nurses' station and down the hall, so I had draped the stethoscope around my neck (like I've watched every other person that actually uses a stethoscope do). From the moment I had that stethoscope on me, I started getting stares. At first, I thought

I was just imagining it. But quickly I realized that people--all people, whether they worked at the hospital or were patients or visitors--actually <u>were</u> treating me differently. "No, no--After you." "Go ahead, you take the elevator, I'll get the next one." I'm fairly certain I nearly got invited into a patient room for assistance.

By the time I made it back to the physician's office down the street, the doctor was pulling into the parking lot. He rolled down his window to thank me for this above-and-beyond favor. Instead of saying, "You're welcome," though, I asked this: "Can you imagine how I was treated when I had that stethoscope around my neck?"

"Yup," he stated simply, "Like a god, huh?"

"No kidding," I replied. "Weirdest situation ever."

As I headed back to my office at the hospital, I realized I liked that feeling. I liked the power. And I started to feel frustration that I no longer had my stethoscope to prove that I was important.

All I have with me is my Bible.

Did I just say that??

Obviously, I still have an awful lot to learn about envy.

ENVY

YARD SALE

Yard sales are popular where I live. Many Saturday mornings at 7:30, I pick up my parents and we head off to find treasures we never knew we needed. We usually return home with nothing (which my mom and I call an unfulfilling trip, but my dad labels a complete success), although every once in a while we'll find that perfect item that we get for next-to-nothing. We have more fun driving around town and talking and laughing than anything else.

Curiously, we rarely find a yard sale that compares to our annual family yard sale. In fact, few of these advertised sales should actually fall into the category of "yard sale"--there aren't enough items. My family has the corner on the yard sale market in the area. And those that know about this event plan their 4th of July holiday around it, because it is huge.

It's due mostly to two older brothers. All year, they gather yard sale items from friends. Both are teachers, so they encourage friends that are cleaning out rooms or garages or are preparing to move to donate their items to his yard sale. One brother, Rod, is willing to store them in his storage shed (he's super-organized, too, so he can pack a ton in that shed), then he sells them and gets the profits. Each of us in the family is also allowed to sell our wares, as long as we price each item and put our name on the item so we get appropriate credit (Rod is also the cashier at the yard sale, and he keeps track down to the penny). And each participant pays a portion of the newspaper ad (which Rod is in charge of).

Like I said, he's really organized.

But here's where his genius really plays out.

The family yard sale is typically held on the first Saturday in July. A hot, hot Saturday. We usually gather between 5 and 6 am, although Rod has probably been up for hours by the time we arrive in the morning. By 1 pm, the sale is typically over. At the end of the sale, we all gather our things that didn't sell, and we either (a) take them back home or (b) take them down to the donation station in town.

Unless we want to choose option C.

By 1:00 pm on a hot July day, we're all pretty exhausted, and often sunburned and ready to go inside and cool off. At the end of the yard sale, Rod offers each participant a third option: don't take our personal items anywhere, but let him take care of them. He will put them all away in his shed and sell them next year.

Here's the glitch: he gets the profit from that item if it sells in the future.

At the end of a long day of working a yard sale, that third option is a cool drink of water. Who wants to spend another couple of hours loading all of those unsold items, driving them to the donation station, and unloading them yet again? Or even more time consuming is the thought of having to take them back home and store them for another year. Most of the time, most of us donate our items to Saint Rod, happy to be rid of our junk.

Until the next year.

When summer rolls around again, and we're ready to start the yard sale, we all peruse the items (because we do almost as much trading with each other as we do selling to the public). Collectively, we are annually shocked at how much of our stuff now has Rod's name on it (and often he doesn't even remove our names from the stickers, just crosses the name off and puts his initials on).

And all of a sudden, I want that item back.

Sure, that piece of junk was useless enough for me to place it in the yard sale in the first place. Sure, it didn't sell the first time (or maybe even the second or third time). But now, now it has Devil Rod's name on it. And it was mine. And it should be mine.

I can't tell you how many times more than one of us have re-purchased our own items because we either found a purpose for the items or we just wanted them to be recognized as ours.

I love watching envy seep into the heart of one of my other brothers as they watch an item be sold that was previously theirs but now has the mark of Rod on it. I can't believe how goofy they look as they grimace when Rod writes the amount sold on his section of the tally paper. They are being so very silly.

Until one of my items that Rod stole is heading to the check-out table.

Envy is a powerful and deadly sin, and it is emphatically illustrated at our yard sale.

I didn't want an item. I intentionally loaded it up and took it to the sale. It wasn't good enough to be purchased during a whole sale, and I didn't care enough about it to even take it back for the next year. It wasn't even important enough to donate to charity. I let Rod have it. And then, a year--or even two--later, someone finally finds a purpose for it, and the twenty-five cents ends up going to my brother.

And I am seething.

It's something that is really easy to spot and mock in one of my brothers. But when it happens to me--watch out!!

How do I combat the envy?

Take a step back and remember. Remember the past and how we got to this moment, where a stranger is now bartering for stuff that is no longer mine but feels like mine. Remember that I'm helping someone find a treasure, when to me that thing was only trash. Remember that this is my brother, who helped me dispose of this in the first place.

Remember that this stuff is only stuff, and the day is about cleaning out, making a little money, and having fun with my family.

I don't typically remember the stuff that I've let go of, until someone else has it. It's time for me to let go a little more, and be grateful that I could give it away.

Lord, forgive my envy.

ENVY
HOW'S YOUR DAY

Few people that know what I do for a living are envious of my life. I am daily surrounded by death, drama, and disease.

Here's one day. It started with a department debriefing--that means something tragic happened that affected staff members or, as in this case, a whole department, so I entered the scene to help walk them through it, let them process it, and listen and help them respond to their needs. Then I dealt with legal issues regarding a patient's recent death and subsequent organ donation. I then went to a couple of meetings, then I had an Ethics consult for a patient on life support (when we aren't sure about a clinical ethics issue, the Bioethics Committee gets a request for a consult. Usually, I get the request and make the consult happen. In this case, we needed to withdraw support, so I got to work with the family to prepare them for that). I then responded to a Code Blue, which meant someone stopped breathing; this someone stopped breathing just as I had sat down for lunch in the cafeteria. An hour later, I returned to my office to find a staff member had taken my lunch (and my now-cold soup bowl) to my office; that was a real gift. I met with a staff member that was struggling with her own issues; I was asked to step into another meeting regarding another staff member. I managed to write up the minutes from the ethics consult before my daughter called home to say she was sick and was going to need to leave early from track practice. I got home in time to let my Hamburger Helper help me make a great meal, then I headed off to church to train a group of deacons.

I know I am right where I should be, serving in a healthcare system that includes a hospital, home health, palliative care, hospice and a hospice house, a cancer center, clinics, and an innovative pediatric center.

And yet, there are days that I envy my girlfriend who doesn't have to work outside the home, so she takes her labradoodle on runs, she plays tennis nearly every day, she can go out to lunch when she wants, and she stays in great shape. Sometimes, I'm more envious of my friend who is a teacher, particularly once summer comes. Every once in a while, I'm envious of my pastor friends, who, while they have to be available for any crisis at any time, they get to spend time--sometimes lots of time--having meetings at their regular Starbucks (which is our modern-day watering hole). Often I look at my friends and I want their lives.

But usually that's because I forget that I'm right where God wants me...even on the difficult days.

Are you right where God wants you? If so, are you working your hardest to be the best you you can be? If not, then what would be your best you?

How was your day?

ENVY
THE FREE GIFT

Years ago, I was walking through the department store one mid-week afternoon, when nobody seemed to be around, and I saw the makeup counter beckoning me with that giant advertisement for *The Free Gift*. Ladies, you know what I mean. Many of us will only purchase our makeup when it is offered with a corresponding "free gift"—which, most assuredly, is not free.

I stood there drooling long enough for a cosmetic professional to come over and help me out. As she was talking to me, I realized that the free gift wasn't something I needed; it was a package full of skin cleansers and other accessories for extremely oily skin, and my skin's not oily. The woman kept talking with me (because I was the only person within 50 yards), so I told her about how I never buy makeup unless there's a free gift involved (which showed how desperately cheap I am; thankfully, she didn't seem to hold that against me), and since this cleanser package wasn't for my skin, I guess I'd better move on... unless, of course, she had any other promotions coming up she might want to tell me about.

I am shameless.

She told me to hang on, and she ducked behind her magic counter.

She disappeared into the cabinet below and soon came up with two big boxes: one was filled with hundreds of lipsticks, and the other was piled high with tubes of face wash. She told me that in order to partake of anything in those shiny grab bags of treasure and delight, I would have to purchase something. So, frantically scanning the area, I grabbed the first thing I could reach--sunscreen! Yes, I need sunscreen! So the cosmetic professional said she'd be able to throw in some lipstick *and* some face wash...free.

I was ecstatic. If you are a man, you may not understand my excitement, and if you are a woman, you may believe my excitement was slightly misplaced, but it's *free makeup*!

As my new best friend was ringing up my purchase, I said, "It must be great being able to have all the makeup you want whenever you want it."

She replied, "Sure, it was pretty neat at first, since they give you so much free stuff. But you'd be surprised how quickly the novelty wears off."

Then (and here's where my misplaced judgment really comes in), I said, "Still, what a great perk. I wish I had a perk like that in my job."

"Well," she said, "You must get some kind of benefit where you work. What do you do?"

"I'm a pastor," I replied.

I'm realizing that I've got to stop admitting the truth quite so often. She looked at me as if I was crazy. She said, "You're kidding me, right? You're wishing you had the perk of a little extra makeup? I'll tell you what, I'd give just about anything to have a better relationship with The Man Upstairs, that's what."

I left the makeup counter in sheepish silence.

As I walked out, I thought about going back and saying, "You *can* have a better relationship with the the Man Upstairs; you don't have to be a pastor. Like this lipstick, that relationship is absolutely free to you." I thought about all the great and spiritual responses I could have given...and didn't.

But I think that scene was meant to be more for me to recognize what I have, not what I don't have. The Lord nudged me well that day, and every time I go to the makeup counter now, I think about that woman, and about the great relationship with The Lord of the universe that I already have, before I start thinking about what makeup I "need."

Since all I "need"...is Him.

ENVY
A DAY IN THE LIFE

Now, I'm not saying it had been a bad day or anything, but...

I started the day by being called in to work at 5:30 am; that is post-shower, but pre-makeup/hair/clothes/get kids out/capture a clue. I had 10 minutes to get ready for the day, because I figured that once I got to work, I'd be staying there for the duration.

Turned out that was the only thing I was right about today.

Let's fast-forward through a high-stress day of trauma to trauma (literally) in the hospital to about 1:00 pm. I had a seminar I was leading at 1:30, so I figured, *Sure, I have plenty of time to kill by doing something brainless: walking around an all-purpose store.*

I should back up and explain that I had just had two total hip replacements, so my mode of walking was to motor (and by "motor," of course I mean "awkwardly stumble") around in a mauve-colored walker. so there's actually nothing fast (or exotic and mysterious) about anything I did.

I meandered through one department, checking out work-out clothes (ah, yes, I remember working out...those were the days), moved to the next area and perused the clearance furniture, then headed to the back of the store for a couple of nuts that I needed to replace the ones that came with the recumbent bike that I bought and had to assemble with what were clearly instructions for filling a swimming pool, because there's no way those instructions--or the nuts and bolts that came with it--actually went to this particular piece of exercise equipment. I got what I thought I would need and will surely return because they're not right, and I headed to the check-out lane. But I had to navigate through a very long aisle that runs from the back of the store to the front. All of a sudden, from behind me, I heard the sound of a shopping cart, getting closer and closer, and faster and faster. A woman pushing the cart blasted past me—she thought she needed to race me (me--with the walker) to the checkout lane! She and the five hundred items in her cart get there about a year before me, but she then decides she's not actually in a hurry, so she takes her sweet little time in emptying the cart onto the counter.

Now I'm late for my next appointment.

But that's not the major issue.

I want all of you that I crossed paths with that day to remind me that we crossed paths. I want you to tell me what you saw. Here's why: in my day of hurrying, I'm not entirely sure when I stopped to use the restroom. But I am praying--oh, how I am praying--that it was when I got out of the car at the store and that's actually when I, somehow, through an unnatural act of nature, got my skirt hiked up all the way in to the back of my tights. I'm hoping it was only as I walked through the many departments of the store that I was flashing everyone behind me, only realizing my predicament when I let vanity strike and peeked at myself as I waddled through the mirror aisle at Fred Meyer. Oh, I'm hoping that I was all put together as I consoled that family, or talked with that patient on the second floor, or went to lunch with someone I've spent decades trying to impress (my now friend and former piano teacher).

Now, I would put this story less in the category of "pride" and more in the category of "I hope I didn't totally humiliate myself today."

Ever have one of those days?

When, oh, when, am I going to be less of a hot mess and more exotic and mysterious? When am I going to take my hair out of a bun and watch it flow like those movie stars, instead of it looking like a stunned animal on my head? When am I going to walk into a room and watch as people admire my gracefulness instead of turn to look because I have six feet of toilet paper trailing behind me?

When, Lord, when?

The immediate answer is: Probably never. Because that's not who I am. Continuing to wish I was someone else diminishes who God made me to be.

Are you wishing you were something other than you are? Instead, let's you and I both commit today to blooming where we are planted, to see what The Lord has blessed us with and use it to become a blessing to others.

I'm in. Are you?

Chapter Three: Gluttony— Popping the Top Button

GLUTTONY
ENOUGH IS ENOUGH

1 Corinthians 3:10-16, The Foundation of Christ

> *By the grace God has given me, I laid a foundation as an
> expert builder, and someone else is building on it. But each
> one should be careful how he builds. For no one can lay
> any foundation other than the one already laid, which is
> Jesus Christ. If any man builds on this foundation using
> gold, silver, costly stones, wood, hay or straw, his work will
> be shown for what it is, because the Day will bring it to
> light. It will be revealed with fire, and the fire will test the
> quality of each man's work. If what he has built survives,
> he will receive his reward. If it is burned up, he will suffer
> loss; he himself will be saved, but only as one escaping
> through the flames. Don't you know that you yourselves are
> God's temple and that God's Spirit lives in you?*

When you think about going to the movies, what gets you more
excited: the prospect of losing yourself in a great plot, or losing yourself
in a great big tub of heaven—er, I mean tub of popcorn?

Yeah, me, too.

When you head to a Mexican restaurant that offers endless baskets
of chips and salsa, do you find that by the time your food arrives at the
table you're no longer hungry...and the waiter has reached his target
heart rate from refilling your perpetually empty basket of chips?

Yeah, me, too.

When you head to one of those warehouse stores, are you more
interested in the great deals...or the free food samples?

Yeah, me, too.

When you put on your jeans, do you wonder how in the world they
got so tight? After all, at the movies, you had zero candy, only popcorn;

at the Mexican restaurant, you ordered only a salad, which you didn't even finish; and at Costco, all you bought was laundry detergent and a 72-pound jar of kalamata olives, which you aren't sure what you'll do with, but it was such a good deal that you can't believe you ever lived without?

Maybe gluttony will hit closer to home than you are expecting.

When you think of a glutton, don't you picture somebody with a complete lack of self-control in their eating habits? I do. The word gluttony is technically defined as habitual eating or drinking to excess. But that's a pretty benign description of gluttony.

A better picture to me is Jabba the Hut from the Star Wars movies; he is what comes to mind when I think about the Deadly Sin of Gluttony.

But there's more to gluttony than food.

Think about this: Gluttony is wanting something to a greater degree than the way God created us to want it, because that want, that desire, sets us up to be alone.

See, we were created to be in relationship—relationship with one another, and relationship with God. Gluttony breaks that relationship, because our focus turns to wanting to find comfort, find peace, find satisfaction in something that isn't a relationship but is completely self-gratifying…and that is the opposite of a relationship. This want makes us more lonely, more unfulfilled, more anxious, and wanting more, and more, and more.

And enough is never enough.

We are made to be content in the Lord. We shouldn't have to be searching for contentment in the things that come across our plates every day. Unfortunately, though, we can all too quickly become gluttonous in nearly anything that comes along--food, activities, people, success, finances, anything. Ever meet a cookie on a counter and feel the need to immediately devour it before it gets away—or before someone else grabs it--and then be absolutely convinced that the only thing that will fill the stomach of the soul is getting another cookie just like it? Ever get a compliment, and realize that it triggers your need, not for doing well, but for getting more compliments? Ever find yourself out at the mall and throwing a little plastic card at any clerk available in order to get the satisfaction that only "retail therapy" seems to be able to give? If you understand that, then you understand the point of gluttony.

As we move into this theme, we'll be addressing this question: *How much is actually enough?*

Nearly anything in excess can lure us away from God instead of leading us toward Him; therefore, gluttony is a deadly sin that marks us for human wants over Godly pursuits. Anything other than that singular focus on a relationship with the Lord and relationship with others will cause us to engorge ourselves and never be full, to shovel it in and never be satisfied, to dive deeper and deeper into the pit of despair and never see daylight again.

God designed the world for us to enjoy, not to indulge in or bulge from. God made such pleasurable things as recreation, and food, and activities like shopping and family outings to be gifts, not to be the driving force that moves us away from the very calling that we have as believers.

So, you might be one of those people saying, "This chapter, I'm off the hook. I may have pride and envy, but I don't overeat." Maybe you should go back and read the chapter on pride once again. Most of us are gluttonous in one way or another. Maybe you just don't know it. We're all driven to want what we want, when we want, in the ways we want. And when those wants cause you to foam at the mouth or to try to find ways to get those things instead of seeking first the kingdom of God, then you've moved to the point of gluttony.

Matthew tells us in chapter 6 to seek first the kingdom of God, and all these things will be added to us. The Apostle Paul remarks in 1 Corinthians, "Declare that you yourself are the temple of the Holy Spirit, so God can be glorified in all that you say and do." In this passage, Paul talks about Christ being the master builder of the temple...and the temple is your body.

Knowing that, ask yourself:

Today, do I find myself indulging in a Snickers, or in the Scripture?

Do I seek with passion after the perfect pair of jeans that will hide my many flaws, or the perfect relationship with the Lord who takes my sins away?

Do I want to whet my whistle with worshiping an athlete, or with worshiping God?

We're taking a long, hard look at gluttony. You get to scrutinize yourself, as you look into your heart and ask how much is really enough. And when you look to Christ instead of looking to your crumbs, you will probably find your answer.

GLUTTONY
TWINKIE

My kids do not understand the power of a Twinkie. And, for a short while, when the Hostess company went out of business (before it was repurchased) I was concerned that future generations may never get the opportunity.

To some of us that are a little older, though, a Twinkie was like a little taste of heaven. One bite into that yellow cake, into that creamy white frosting, and you've got a virtual party in your mouth.

Some of us reminisce as if it was an old friend.

As a kid, I had no idea that that lovely bit of yumminess was made up of some flour, some sugar, and bucketloads of whipped lard…oh, yeah, and lots and lots of preservatives.

Rumors concerning the shelf-life of a Twinkie run rampant: one such story declared that all Twinkies in existence came from the one original batch that was made in 1930. Not true. Another stated that the plastic around the Twinkie would disintegrate before the food inside. Also false. Even the more oft-cited version that a Twinkie had a shelf life of 7 years is incorrect. The official skinny on the life span of a Twinkie is that it will stay fresh for 25 days (which doesn't seem very long when compared to 7 years or infinite, but for a baked good, that is a long time!).

I thought the 7-year duration was a long time. But the fact is I never could even test the 25-day story, because Twinkies never lasted in our house 25 hours. Maybe they fared better at your house.

Are you one of those that could picture yourself diving into a Twinkie as if it's manna and will turn to mold if it stays on the shelf for more than a day?

To the Twinkie-lovers of the world, think about this: Why is it so easy to frantically indulge in something that has a fairly substantial shelf-life, while we take our Bibles and let them sit on a shelf for days or weeks or even years?

In Paul's day, the people in Corinth were arguing about who was the greater speaker—some said that they were followers of the great Apollos, others claimed Paul, and still others Cephas. But Paul was urging them toward seeking after Christ, not as their speaker or teacher, but as their Savior. The apostles—Peter, Paul, and the others—were nothing more than Twinkies in the grand scheme of things. Perhaps these greats settled the spirit for a moment, but the goal wasn't to highlight them; it was to highlight God.

Maybe you aren't a Twinkie lover. Maybe you overdo it in the Snickers or the Doritos of life. The point is that we are more prone to indulge in things that are tasty for a moment, as we put on the shelf the thing that has greater value. If we'll seek after Jesus, we'll discover that He is the real thing, and He will satisfy like no Twinkie ever could.

The Psalmist writes in Psalm 34:8—*Oh, taste and see that the Lord is good. Blessed is the man who takes refuge in Him.*

Something has to be put on the shelf.

What will it be?

GLUTTONY
PUNISHING

I'm not really sure how my parents made ends meet when we were kids. My three brothers and I have never been what you might call "light eaters." My mom didn't typically keep brand-name snacks in the house, because they didn't stay in the house very long. We didn't often have soda pop on the premises, because it was gone almost as soon as it hit the refrigerator (which may explain why, for a time, as an adult I kept an actual, fully stocked pop machine in my garage).

I also vividly remember the times we went out to a restaurant to eat, because, even though we were all involved in sports, we seemed to constantly eat as if we were carbo-loading for tomorrow's big game.

I do, however, recall a particular trip to our town's all-you-can-eat buffet restaurant. It was my first experience at such an eating establishment, where, once Dad and Mom paid and we walked through the turnstile, we were welcome to fill our plates like mountains...and go back as many times as we wanted. Soda flowed like water, a soft-serve ice cream machine beckoned children to attempt to create the world's largest sundae, and the tables and tables of steamy, deep-fried, gravy-laden food seemed never-ending.

Never before have my eyes been bigger than my stomach...until that day. I started with dessert and four glasses of soda. I cleaned my plate and moved on to chicken strips and a Matterhorn of fries. I was holding off for the piece de resistance: a platter of mashed potatoes completely covered with the kind of gravy my Mom never liked us to have. Funny, I don't recall there being any vegetables in the restaurant, but my Mom's one plate, only half-full, was a beautiful if sparse array of greens (and she never went back). I couldn't figure out why she didn't want to get her money's worth.

What I most remember, though, was the picture of my two older brothers, Tim and Rod. They were singularly focused on the deep-fried shrimp. I could barely see their faces, for they were surrounded by mounds of shrimp. But they each had a well-organized place setting: a vat of cocktail sauce directly in front of them, heaping plate of deep-fried shrimp at the twelve o'clock spot, a bowl of shrimp tail remains at three o'clock, and a pile of deep-fried batter remains at nine o-clock.

They worked like machines, methodically grabbing a shrimp, efficiently peeling the fried portion off and dropping it at nine o'clock, dipping the now-naked shrimp into the cocktail sauce, biting the shrimp off at the tail, then disposing the tail at three o'clock...and repeating the process. It was mesmerizing to watch.

I asked them why they weren't eating the battered part. Without looking up, my oldest brother Tim, never missing a beat, methodically stated, "Why waste calories?"

Were calories an issue at this point?

After about a half-hour of this impressive show, I noticed that Rod was starting to slow down his shrimp machine. My dad noticed it at about the same time I did. Dad, head shaking, asked Rod, "How are you doing?"

Rod replied, "Getting full."

Then he added, "Better eat faster."

Eventually, we rolled out of the buffet and groaned all the way home. Both boys were sick within an hour, but by night-time, they were back to the kitchen, opening the fridge to see if there was anything they could midnight-snack on.

They were my heroes that day.

I can see why my folks rarely took us out to eat. Maybe they thought they would teach us a lesson by taking us to an all-you-can-eat buffet ("If they eat until they're sick, perhaps they'll see that engorging themselves isn't as fun as they thought it could be"). Unfortunately, all it taught us was there there were certain magical restaurants that let you eat until you burst.

Here's the point: My parents gave us a very special treat in taking us out to dinner. Meanwhile, I remember zero of the conversations we had during this time. I don't recall any emotions (other than the drive to get to the next food faster). I can't even tell you how my food tasted, because I shoveled it in as fast as my hands could fly in a singular effort to move on to the next plate.

This story was an eye-opener for me, because through it I learned that gluttony isn't about what I'm eating. It's about trying to feel satisfied, and being afraid that, if I don't grab and consume everything around me, someone might get it--and be satisfied--instead.

Problem is, I can't ever be satisfied by food. In fact, the more I eat, the more I realize that fact, because, like my brothers, I eventually just get sick.

You'd think I would have learned a little sooner.

GLUTTONY

THE MIRACLE FOOD

You know who you are. When food was divided into four groups, you created a fifth. When food became a pyramid, you placed one right at the top. It is a staple. You believe you could live on it, as you live for it.

Chocolate.

Maybe you take your poison, your passion, your chocolate with a glass of wine. Or, perhaps it comes melted on a sundae. Then again, it might be wrapped in aluminum foil and surrounding a hazelnut, or perhaps it has a candy coating and the insignia M&M stamped on it.

Chocolate. It's everywhere. It's an obsession. Some of us live for it. When you are depressed, maybe you grab an Almond Joy bar. When seeking a snack on the sly, perhaps you sneak a Snickers. When wanting an aphrodisiac, maybe it's Dove chocolate or Ferraro Rocher. Chocolate runs the gamut between the plain snack and the award-winning work of art.

Ever grab a bite before a race? These days, there are endless power-bar possibilities. But it used to be that we would grab a candy bar and expect it to get us across the finish line. It's typically at the 5-mile point—when that cramp in my side sets in—that I ever remember that it takes more than a candy bar to win.

Why do I seem to seek the sugary solutions, and try to make them my foundation for living? In 1 Corinthians 3:10-11 we read: *By the grace God has given me, I laid a foundation as an expert builder, and someone else is building on it. But each one should be careful how he builds. For no one can lay any foundation other than the one already laid, which is Jesus Christ.*

See, the people of Corinth were more interested in showing off how "spiritual" they were by claiming which apostle they were connected with than in establishing a true life in Christ. We do the same thing-- finding the wrong thing to place our hopes and our peace on.

Sad? Go shopping—maybe this time retail therapy will be the key to happiness.

Lonely? Grab a chocolate—maybe this time it will satisfy the soul.

The imitations become the foundation that we all too often come to rely on as building blocks. Sadly, those are the very things that become stumbling blocks, moving us away from the firm foundation of The Lord.

Let's be clear. Nobody's saying chocolate isn't great. It's wonderful. But can one be truly sustained with chocolate? Some of us think so.

1 Peter 2:1-3 says it well:

> *Therefore, rid yourselves of all malice and all deceit, hypocrisy, envy, and slander of every kind (and gluttonous acts). Like newborn babies, crave pure spiritual milk, so that by it you may grow up in your salvation, now that you have tasted that the Lord is good.*

One very real problem is that what we grab is not spiritual milk, but chocolate milk.

Give me Jesus. And occasionally, sneak in a Snickers. Don't do it the other way around. It's not worth it.

GLUTTONY
THE ROAD TO HELL IS PAVED WITH AMERICAN INTENTIONS

Here's one definition of gluttony: an inordinate desire to consume more than that which one requires.

I don't really like that definition.

Probably because it's a little too close to home. Do I need that four-dollar latte? Well, no, but a treat every once in a while is nice.

That's probably not gluttony.

Do I need that latte every day?

Hey, now, I need coffee to start my day, you know. And I don't always have time to make a pot at home. And that coffee stand is on the way. And come afternoon, I need a little pick-me-up. Wow, I just moved from thinking coffee is a special treat to rationalizing it as a need. I'm treading on thin and gluttonous ice.

We should probably change the subject from coffee. We should talk about overexercising. I can talk about that all day long and not get defensive. Wonder why?

Why is more money spent in diet centers than spent in ministries? That says a lot about where we are as a people group.

We are consumers. We consume natural resources, we consume the latest and greatest fads. We are in an epidemic of American proportion. Have you ever ventured to guess how much we in America spend on looking good? Whether it's in weight-loss programs, department stores buying the right clothing, makeup counters buying the perfect eyeliner, getting all the right tools, or eating everything in sight to get to "the perfect bite," Gluttony truly expands beyond one who overeats; it's just that food is the most obvious topic.

Go to your bathroom. No, seriously, go. I can wait. Now—Look inside your vanity (why do you think it's called that?) and see how much makeup or cologne you have that you'll never use. Look in your closet and see how much clothing you have that won't be—or will barely be—worn. Look in your cupboard and see how many canned goods you are saving for the next flood.

What drives you: looking good to society, or looking good to Jesus?

GLUTTONY
QUARTER–POUNDERS

Remember your first trip to McDonald's? I couldn't finish my first Big Mac (but, with lots of practice, I became quite accomplished at downing it). The hamburgers used to come with a small fry and a medium drink, and it was considered an enormous meal. It was satisfying. It was filling.

But today, that small fry seems so small. In my family, we only get the small fry as a snack to go with a diet beverage (wouldn't want to waste calories on a full-sugar soda). In order to make a satisfying meal, it takes a medium or large fry to go along with the Quarter Pounder and an apple pie with my diet beverage.

Let's be honest: The bigger the fry order, the better.

Unfortunately, we're super-sizing our lives like we're super-sizing our meals. Having a car isn't enough; it has to be the right car. Having a coat for winter and shorts for summer isn't enough; we have to have the right clothes. And not just a roof over our heads, but the right house in the right neighborhood. We seem to be super-sizing our lives away.

The folks over at Veggie Tales got it right when Madame Blueberry, who had everything she needed (and most of what she wanted) couldn't be satisfied. But then the giant Stuff-Mart opened up in the neighborhood, promising joy and satisfaction to those who buy, buy, buy. It's a lesson in thankfulness, and it doesn't come easily to Madame Blueberry.

And she's a cartoon.

Most of the world's resources and wealth are centered in one little spot on the globe: North America. Think about how much food Americans throw away each day, when people in third-world countries beg for a bowl of rice with a few beans.

May God forgive me in my gluttony.

When I was a kid, my parents promised our family of six a road trip from Washington State down to California. Disneyland. So my dad did something super-creative: he opened up the attractive wood paneling on the wall, he set a glass jar inside the wall, then he closed up the paneling and cut a slit in the wood. For months, we put all of our extra coins into the wall in order to fund that trip. It was fun to find change and push it into the wall. In the first weeks, we could hear coins clinking against the glass of the jar. But pretty soon, the sound became muffled, as the jar got full and coins were hitting coins and dropping down onto the wood. When Dad opened the paneling back up, money *poured* out of the wall.

And that was just from our extra change.

Well, to be honest, it was also from the several—and I mean *several*—silver dollars that he filled the jar, and the wall, with.

What's more, my folks then let us use that money to make our budget for the trip. We kids decided how much to spend for meals, what choices we made for extras, how the consequences of one action came out later. What a great lesson.

What if I intentionally decided to do something simple: instead of ordering a medium fry, start getting a small fry, then take the money from every medium fry that I would have gotten (about a dollar), and set it aside in my own little hidden jar? Then, at the end of the year, I count it all and give it away? What if you and I each picked our own personal goal, whether it's with fries, or chocolate, or coffee?

Imagine: What would happen if we all bought one less latte, one less super-sized meal, one less frock, one less piece of jewelry, one less can of tennis balls, one less diet soda (diet soda?? No, no, anything but that!!), and we gave that savings to those who were hungry?

Oh, what a difference that could make--in the world, and in me (and my waistline as an added bonus).

GLUTTONY
THE QUICK FIX

We're pretty obsessed with the quick fix.

Gain too much weight? Get the fat sucked out.

Unhappy in marriage? Get a divorce.

Find yourself depressed? Take a pill.

Want to drown your sorrows? Have a drink.

Need an answer? If you can't get it in 1.3 seconds on the internet, it just may not be a question worth asking.

We're in an era of the fast fix. But that's not how God made us. God created us to be on a journey, where every day is an adventure. He created tasty food and beautiful sights and twists and turns along the way, to be more of an experience and less of a frantic goal of hurrying up to get to the next thing.

Food, like anything, can be gifts God has given in order to enjoy the One who created us. But they can also become the obstacles that move us more away from Him than toward Him. We can tell the difference when those objects become the things we live for, instead of living for the Lord.

Paul writes in 1 Corinthians 3:11-13:

> *For no one can lay any foundation other than the one already laid, which is Jesus Christ. If any man builds on this foundation using gold, silver, costly stones, wood, hay, or straw (or Twinkies, and more), his work will be shown for what it is, because the Day will bring it to light. It will be revealed with fire, and the fire will test the quality of each man's work.*

There's a story you just may know: The Three Little Pigs. I had to verify the story with a certain five-year-old in the vicinity to make sure I had it right. One pig builds a house with straw, and a second one makes one using sticks, and they quickly get their houses done and move in and move on. Meanwhile, the third pig has been working hard as he builds his house with bricks. While the other 2 piglets are dancing and prancing around, the third piglet spends his time sweating over building a house that is solid—a house on a firm foundation. The first two piglets saw themselves as more practical and smarter and moving on with real living, because they got their job done quickly...right up until the wolf huffed and puffed and blew the houses down. We all know where the first two pigs went (depending on the version you read): to the one who built the house on the rock—the house of bricks. That was the house the wolf could not destroy.

What are you building your house upon? Sticks and straw, or the solid rock of Christ? Can you relate to the two men who left Jerusalem on the way to Emmaus? They were so consumed by their own heartache and problems that they never saw the person who was walking with them.

Jesus.

When we go for the quick-fix to satisfy what only Jesus can satisfy, we will see our houses easily blown down when the world around us huffs and puffs. After all, how much time does it take to down a Twinkie? How big is a Quarter-Pounder? How long does that perfect bottle of perfume last? Or one's savings?

Be honest. Are you trying to live for the momentary *ahhhh* that comes from that stuff, or do you want to be on an eternal ride, a continuous journey with the One who satisfies the longings of your heart? Let's choose to be a people who find more happiness in Jesus than in the food that we eat, the clothes that we wear, and the things that we buy.

I'm ready...are you?

Let's take the ride together.

GLUTTONY
INNER PEACE

What's your poison for inner peace? Is it buying that tool, or ordering that outfit, or bidding on that auction item? Perhaps the quickest way to get a little comfort is in a little comfort food.

Some people like sweets. Ice cream, or chocolate, or ice cream and chocolate. Others like to carbo-load. Me—I like savory snacks. And the saltier, the better.

My favorite snack these days, my quickest comfort, comes in a beautiful see-through package, and it's readily available at every grocery store in town. I know this. It is the Hint of Lime Tostito, and it is good. Have you ever had these? These chips are tasty. But every chip does not hold within it the perfect bite. Not every chip in this package makes the grade as the ultimate comfort chip. Only a select few actually pass as the chip of immediate gratification.

See, these tortilla chips have a lime-flavored salt on them, but not every chip is doused in it. Inside the bag can be found only about eight or nine perfect chips, where the green salt covers the whole chip. I spent $3.29 on this bag recently. Very recently. I used to buy a bag on Tuesdays and take it to our staff meeting. While everyone else was eating a lovely lunch, I'd be digging through the bag in search of that perfect chip. I'd make an alliance with whoever's sitting next to me, convincing them to eat the other chips so I wouldn't have to bother with those calories. And once I got to the perfect chip, and taste it, mmm, I'm satisfied. Completely.

Problem is, my quick delight turns to dismay even more quickly. The chip is gone. The taste is gone. The memory is quickly fading.

Better find another chip. Better eat some of the less-than-perfect chips on the way, too, even though they won't taste as good, because at least they're something. Eventually, I get to the bottom of the bag. And a few minutes later, I'm no better off than when I started…except that now I need to go work out, too, which is even more depressing.

Oh, taste and see that the Lord is good, the Psalmist declares (34:8). He's not talking about Tostitos; he talking about God.

God uses the things around us all the time to show us how much greater He is, and how much bigger His blessings are, and how much more He loves us than we can imagine. My Hint of Lime Tostitos taste pretty good. But when they're gone, maybe, just maybe, this time I'll remember that The Lord is even better.

GLUTTONY
THE CHALLENGE

The boys in my house love to be boys. They watch action movies. They tease each other. They compete in burping (and other) contests. They eat every bit of junk food they can get their teeth into and try to justify every item's nutritional value. For example: York Peppermint Patties have mint in them. Mint is an herb, which is practically a vegetable—hence, a Peppermint Patty is a vegetable. You probably already know the line of thinking concerning milk chocolate (made from milk—there's your dairy—and the cocoa bean, a bean, is, again, a vegetable). Pizza is the ultimate health food: crust...flour...wheat...grains; cheese is dairy; tomatoes are as healthy as they come; pepperoni is a strength-building protein—need I continue?

When there is a task to be accomplished, like trim the bushes or head to the dump, they motivate themselves by planning a reward for their hard work. The reward usually has something to do with a gallon-size Slurpee and an order of nachos from 7-Eleven [you just don't get it Mom—you *have* to get the nachos, because the chili and the cheese are free, so we really have no choice but to dump as much gunk on top of the chips (here's what I don't get: they end up having to also buy a pack of Tums in order to make it through the evening after they've "worked" hard enough to reward themselves, so where the words "free" or "reward" come in, I'm not really sure)].

It's pretty easy to justify gluttony.

I _have_ to get this 5-gallon size jug of soda, Mom, because it's a much better deal than one that a normal human can properly consume.

Remember, Mom, the chili and cheese are _free_.

I need to try to eat this whole batch of chocolate chip cookie dough batter; you never know when cookie dough may come my way again.

A tough thing about gluttony--food addiction--is that you can't just give it up cold turkey (figuratively) like you can another addiction. The more food you consume, the more gluttony consumes you. It can become the thing you focus on more than anything else, and it's hard to get your mind off of it, since you don't have to look far to see someone doing exactly what you want to do: eat.

I rarely eat to satisfy my hunger. I regularly eat to satisfy my soul. I eat for sport. I would qualify for the Food Olympics. My eyes are never bigger than my stomach.

Exercising moderation is the key; praying that The Lord will keep my attention away from the deep fryer and on His plans for me is something I battle nearly every waking hour of the day.

But I want my body to be His temple. I want to be healthy so I can live a long life in thankful service to God.

Food issues may not be your issue, but I'm guessing that you could take out the word "food" and insert something you struggle with, something that you are gluttonous over.

Together, let's place our struggles at the foot of the Cross, give them to The Lord, and rise up and walk away and NOT take them back.

In the words of my boys: I challenge you.

CHAPTER FOUR: LUST—IT'S NOT AS PRIVATE AS YOU THINK

LUST

CAUTION: DANGEROUS READING AHEAD

John 4:1-26, Jesus and the Samaritan Woman

The Pharisees heard that Jesus was gaining and baptizing more disciples than John, although in fact it was not Jesus who baptized, but his disciples. When the Lord learned of this, he left Judea and went back once more to Galilee.

Now he had to go through Samaria. So he came to a town in Samaria called Sychar, near the plot of ground Jacob had given to his son Joseph. Jacob's well was there, and Jesus, tired as he was from the journey, sat down by the well. It was about the sixth hour.

When a Samaritan woman came to draw water, Jesus said to her, "Will you give me a drink?" (His disciples had gone into the town to buy food.)

The Samaritan woman said to him, "You are a Jew and I am a Samaritan woman. How can you ask me for a drink?" (For Jews do not associate with Samaritans.)

Jesus answered her, "If you knew the gift of God and who it is that asks you for a drink, you would have asked him and he would have given you living water."

"Sir," the woman said, "you have nothing to draw with and the well is deep. Where can you get this living water? Are you greater than our father Jacob, who gave us the well and drank from it himself, as did also his sons and his flocks and herds?"

Jesus answered, "Everyone who drinks this water will be thirsty again, but whoever drinks the water I give him will never thirst. Indeed, the water I give him will become in him a spring of water welling up to eternal life."

The woman said to him, "Sir, give me this water so that I won't get thirsty and have to keep coming here to draw water."

He told her, "Go, call your husband and come back."

"I have no husband," she replied.

Jesus said to her, "You are right when you say you have no husband. The fact is, you have had five husbands, and the man you now have is not your husband. What you have just said is quite true."

"Sir," the woman said, "I can see that you are a prophet. Our fathers worshiped on this mountain, but you Jews claim that the place where we must worship is in Jerusalem."

Jesus declared, "Believe me, woman, a time is coming when you will worship the Father neither on this mountain nor in Jerusalem. You Samaritans worship what you do not know; we worship what we do know, for salvation is from the Jews. Yet a time is coming and has now come when the true worshipers will worship the Father in spirit and truth, for they are the kind of worshipers the Father seeks. God is spirit, and his worshipers must worship in spirit and in truth."

The woman said, "I know that Messiah" (called Christ) "is coming. When he comes, he will explain everything to us."

Then Jesus declared, "I who speak to you am he."

Those deadly sins.

When we studied the first Deadly Sin, pride, were you surprised at your reaction? *What?? I might actually have that?* I know I acted that way. But, to be forthright, I'll admit that pride is a sin that hit me harder than I expected.

After that came envy. That Deadly, while being easier to admit generally, is harder to discuss when it comes to specifics.

Sure, I have envy. We all have envy.
What do I envy? You want to know <u>really</u>?
Oops, gotta go!

Next came gluttony. Several years ago, when I worked on a sermon series on the Seven Deadlies, the week on gluttony had a great illustration that didn't come until after the service. I had placed a load of snacks—sweet, salty, gooey, rich snacks—on the Communion table, where everyone had the opportunity to stare at them for an hour. Once the worship service got over, I carried those bags back into the church office. You would not believe how many people followed me to break into all the food! Gluttony seems a more easy-to-identify Deadly. Nobody wants it, certainly, but hey, we all get hungry, right?

But then there's this one. During that same sermon series, some of us wanted to be sure not to invite a friend to worship that week. Some of us (okay, me) wouldn't have shown at all ourselves, for fear that this Deadly might reveal me just a little too much.

And yet, we're intrigued by the side show of these sins no less than that wicked car wreck, with its four police cars, two ambulances, and a fire truck that we drive slowly by on an otherwise boring trip over the mountains.

We can't help but be curious…but only from a distance.

This Deadly is a tough subject to broach. We can try to split hairs to explain away our feelings, but the fact is that if we deny that we think about it, then we probably start thinking about not thinking about it, then we start to actually think about it, and then, well, there we are, back to it.

It gets under the skin. It can affect relationships. It can affect time. It can complicate work. And we'd rather just not talk about it, or read about it, but instead go along thinking we're pretty good Christians, so let's just leave it at that.

Look over your shoulder before you read on. This may feel like a movie you shouldn't be watching, a romance novel you shouldn't be reading, or a person you shouldn't be staring at.

You just may get caught, as you study the Deadly Sin (glance both ways) of *lust.*

Shhhhhh.

LUST

THE REAL THING

A few years ago, I did something that somehow changed me in a very real way. If I'm honest, I have to admit that I fought this for some time before actually taking the plunge. It was dramatic, it was costly, it has come with some surprisingly intense pain, and I think that I can say that, in the beginning, anyway, it was worth it.

I had my nails done.

If you had seen my fingernails anytime in the past few decades before the big transformation, and then you saw the "after" hands, you would know in a heartbeat that they were not my real nails; they were imitations. My own nails—I don't bite them or pick them or anything, it's just that I'm sort of rough on them, so they've never really looked very feminine. But those beautiful, perfectly groomed, perfectly colored things—they're something else. And I found it so interesting that 10 little pieces of acrylic could do something to my attitude. I looked at them, and I wanted to be a little more feminine. They made me want to stand a little straighter and even, at times, act a little bit more like an adult.

All because of something fake.

And I got to thinking that, along with my nails, I go for a lot of imitation in my own little world.

Imitation fingernails. Imitation mayonnaise—in my family, terrific arguments have ensued in the Great Mayonnaise vs. Miracle Whip Debate…I won't begin to go into it. Imitation glass. Imitation wood. Imitation milk. Imitation crab—you know, crab with a K? Imitation curls. Imitation hair. Imitation height, with heels, lifts, et cetera. And the list goes on and on.

A couple found each other late in life. They got married, and on that first night, they each went into the bathroom. She took off her wig, her makeup, and her fake eyelashes, and he took off his toupee and his teeth; then they looked up, and they didn't recognize the other person!

Remember that scene from "Anne of Green Gables" that I mentioned earlier--the one in the "Envy" chapter, where Anne replies, "Imitation is the sincerest form of flattery"? When we imitate something, it is because we want to be like, or look like, someone. It can be a sign of respect, a sign that the person we want to imitate is doing something right, and, when it is from the heart, it is a selfless gesture, for it's as much about the other person as it is about me.

When it comes from envy, however, it's lust.

We tend to rely heavily on the wrong sorts of imitations to make us feel better, make us look better, make us happy. We seem to think that in doing particular things, or looking a particular way, we will find peace. And sometimes we do get that result, but only for a moment, because it's a fleeting peace, brought on by something that's not real—because at the heart, we're looking to imitations to somehow transform us.

That's at the heart of lust.

Lust is about momentary pleasure, about something fake, about looking all around in the quest for the perfect whatever, all the while tripping over God in order to try to figure it out. The Lord is right there in the midst of the manicure, trying to whisper in my ear: *I love you. My love is enough.* He's at the shopping mall, looking at all of my bags with names of fancy stores etched on the front, and He's tapping me on the shoulder: *You don't need all of this to be happy.* He's sitting next to you as you watch that program, or you drool over that person, or you think that your heart will explode if you don't get "that" (whatever that is) right now: *You're selling yourself short. I can meet all of your needs, if you'll just let me.*

Now, I'm not knocking particular activities—many are benign unto themselves. Manicures aren't the sin. Neither is what the hairdressers or the shopping malls provide. But when your goal is to find true satisfaction from them, you'll find that they will never be enough. They are all cheap imitations.

Just for a moment, think about the imitations in your own life—the things you have or the things that you do to try to bring about true peace. You may be surprised how many you find.

How about trying something different? After all, Coca-Cola isn't the real thing.

Jesus is.

LUST
ON A PIGGY-BACK RIDE

You know how fun it was when you were a kid. You'd run really fast, then take a giant leap and land on the back of a grownup. Then the adult would gallop around the yard, or stride down the hall of the mall, or hoist you even higher to those broad shoulders so that you could see almost beyond the horizon.

The piggy-back ride.

Maybe you've been the kid on the ride of your life. Maybe you've been the adult doing the hoisting, the galloping, and the striding. Or, maybe you know what it is from watching others.

Did you know it's actually a real term in life beyond preschool? To "piggy-back" means to be fixed to, carried by, or connected with something else. That makes sense, since it's absolutely impossible to have, or to give, a piggy-back ride without two parties: the piggy, and the back. Neither can go it alone. If they try, it's just called walking.

It's the same with lust.

Lust is not something that stands on its own. It's not like pride; I can be proud and jump to other sins, but I don't have to start with another sin in order to have pride. I can be a glutton, but I don't have to be proud first in order to be gluttonous.

Lust is different. It piggy-backs on another sin. Lust is a desire to gratify the senses...immediately. Lust is craving to seek after something that will give me pleasure. Lust is about wanting something that I don't have.

Typically, that something is something that someone else does or has.

And that's where the piggy-backing comes in, for lust finds its root in the Deadly Sin of envy. It's pretty easy to become envious of what we don't have, or envious of what someone else does have, to the point that it rapidly feeds the sin of lust.

Once again, as we've seen with all the other Deadlies, lust is super self-centered. In lusting, I care only about myself—and what I want.

Now.

Right now.

In order to deal with the sin of lust, we have to peel it away and recognize that we're also dealing with envy.

Jesus was talking with the Samaritan woman. This woman clearly struggled with the lust of the flesh (she's had five husbands, and she's currently living with a man to whom she's not married). How easy it would be to dismiss her as a lost cause, an unclean and irredeemable human. But Jesus didn't do that.

Neither should we.

What do you think she was really seeking in all those relationships? Do you wonder if she was envious of something that she didn't have, like the perfect husband, so she went to one after another? Or, maybe she was jealous of what others had, thinking the grass is always greener, so she took from others in an attempt to gain it herself.

Oh, the seeds of lust sprout and bloom so quickly. A look sprouts into a desire, a longing grows into an obsession, and a fixation blooms into action. And then, before you know it, lust has overtaken the whole garden of life.

The curious thing is this: once the lust is satisfied, then the desire for that specific thing dissipates. But what is replaced is an even stronger longing for more of that feeling of satisfaction, and lust begins again.

That's because lust never gets us what we truly long for. Lust only shows us what we think will satisfy us for the moment.

Jesus knew all that. He knew what the Samaritan woman really longed for. He told her, "If you knew the gift of God and who it is that asks you for a drink, you would have asked him and he would have given you living water." He knew that He could offer her a water that satisfied more than a quick quenching of a desire could.

As I keep my focus on the Lord, something happens. My heart and my attitudes begin to change.

In my growing up years (I'm not really sure I've finished that ride), we used to go to Winchell's after church. Oh, the smell of freshly made donuts, with goo dripping from them. Now, with a family our size (and appetites to rival a football team), we were each allowed one donut—one of the regular-sized donuts.

Was I ever envious of those people who could walk in, plunk their change on the counter, and walk away with a bear claw, or a fritter, or a filled donut, while all I had was a measly ol' honey glazed donut with a hole in the middle.

Lust enters so quickly and so painfully, leading me to forget the good thing I have and go after the thing I don't.

Here's what's curious: Honestly, within probably less than 10 minutes of leaving Winchell's, the thought of a donut was the farthest thing from my mind.

By then, I found other things to lust after, other things to become envious of.

Jesus offers us living water. We don't have to be envious, and we don't have to lust after it. All we have to do is ask, and God gives it to us freely, and fills our hearts to the point that we no longer have to focus on those quick-fixes, those material things, the stuff that we must have right now. Instead, we have a real opportunity to want the thing we get to keep, both now and forevermore: the things of Jesus.

Piggy-back on Him today. He'll really take you places.

LUST

IT'S NOT A GAME

Television has changed drastically in the last few years. Reality shows have brought us into an era where more and more people are not only grabbing for the spotlight, but willing to mow down anyone between them and fame...and money.

"Survivor" was one of the first of this new era. "Fear Factor" was another wild show that tested not only the personal fears of contestants, but the stomachs of those who watched, as participants were judged on their ability to balance and deal with heights, their athleticism, and the gross-factor (as they would have to eat things living and dead that no one should ever have to watch, much less consume). Dating reality shows brought couples together in unrealistic settings and then left us to be frustrated when the couple couldn't survive real dating in real life. We have shows that follow the lives of the rich and famous, the rich and obnoxious, and those living in the swamp and the shore.

Like inching past a car crash on the freeway, we are mesmerized to see how these characters will fare under extreme situations and their opposition.

Oh, yes, and the winners often get lots and lots of cash.

Lust is the devil's attempt to get us into an unreal environment--to be out for Number One. It's not so tough to get to a place where you're focusing so strongly on getting this one thing that nothing else matters.

Contestants on these shows are willing to miss out on their real lives and the things that matter because they are convinced that being on the show will get them a better life than being at home. Contestants have missed out on the births of their own children and the deaths of their own family members, thinking that staying on the show would be more beneficial to their lives than their actual lives. It's a decision that has rarely panned out. In fact, these shows have played a role in breaking relationships, dissolving marriages, and leading toward tragedy...including suicide.

"But it's my one chance..."

That phrase is heard regularly on these shows.

Even the extremely popular talent shows promote this unhealthy attitude. Contestants believe that if that one celebrity isn't in shock and awe over the talent of a stranger (who has 90 seconds to wow and woo them), then it's their last chance at a career.

90 seconds.

Wow.

What a lot of pressure we put on ourselves.

In order to be famous.

In order to be singled out.

In order to be special.

In order to matter.

The challenge for you today is to recognize that you *do* matter. You don't have to be recognized as the one best singer, best chef, best model. Just be *your* best, so that when you get to the end of your life and you are standing before The Lord, He judges you with these words: "Well done, good and faithful servant."

That's the only show that counts.

Laurel Jackson

LUST
INDULGENCE

I remember when the movie came out in the theaters. I was surprised it ever made it to the big screen, much less made it to my home town. You probably didn't see it, because it was gone in the blink of an eye. It was the movie "Luther."

Each year, we hear a lot about Martin Luther King, Jr., a man who fought valiantly, and peaceably, for freedom. But not as many people know about King's namesake, Martin Luther, who also fought peaceably for freedom, only freedom of a different kind: Luther's freedom was a freedom for faith. He was a major player in the Protestant Reformation, and the movie is his story.

This film was profound for me. I watched the history of this man, who was already a monk, but who had not yet studied the Bible (which seemed so contradictory). Once he began, finally, to read it, his life was transformed, for he discovered that the religion he lived under was not the same thing as the Jesus he wanted to live for. As he read—for the first time—the book of Romans, he discovered that he was not in charge, and the church was not in charge; his master was Christ, and his relationship with his Master came first.

See, the problem of the church in Luther's day—at least one of the problems—was that the church leaders thought they were in charge, and they searched out ways to please themselves and their church. In Luther's day, the 16th century, people could pay to be officially pardoned for their sins; that pardon was called an indulgence. So, this indulgence, this favor, was given to a person upon payment of cash. At the time, the proceeds from this enormous fund-raiser were used to build St. Peter's Church in Vatican City. It became quite a building campaign.

The Christian leaders of the day took their eyes off Christ. They were more interested in their own pleasure—to build something themselves that would highlight what they had done for the sake of religion (see the Old Testament story of the Tower of Babel for similar insights)—instead of understanding that true joy, and eternal pleasure, comes from The Lord. In their freedom, they thought they were in charge, and were free to enslave the Christian world into having to pay cash in order to have their sins forgiven.

That's what lust gets us. We think we can get away with whatever we're doing, especially if we put it in a particular package—like a package of "the end justifies the means," or a package of "you don't quite understand, but if you truly did, you would agree with me," or a package of religion (not that anybody would ever actually do that).

Usually, though, lust is wrapped up in a secret package, and we hope nobody will ever find it.

But God knows all our hiding places.

I don't say that to try to make you think that God is lurking behind every corner, waiting to "get" you. No, in fact, we are typically the ones lurking, hoping to not get caught. God is actually looking to rescue, to redeem, to give grace, and to bring you back to Him.

All because He cares about you.

That's the difference between lust and love: lust is selfish, and love is selfless.

Which would you like today?

LUST

STIRRING THE POT...OF BISCUITS

I got home at 5:00, knowing I had a 6:15 meeting that evening. I love to cook; it's cathartic. On this dark and rainy day, I thought a quick homemade chicken noodle soup and some biscuits would be easy to make. Of course, it took longer than I thought. I knew I needed to leave by 5:45, so when 5:42 came along and the biscuits were still in the oven, I called to my husband, who was watching hockey on television in the living room, and asked him to take the biscuits out of the oven in five minutes. His reply was, "Uh-huh."

I wasn't thoroughly convinced he'd heard me.

"Honey, now in four minutes, would you please take the biscuits out of the oven?"

Still staring at the screen, he replied, "Sure, do you want me to stir them?"

Uh...stir them?

"I'm leaving now, don't forget the biscuits. I set the timer for you."

"Okay. What biscuits?"

I mumbled and grumbled as I got in the car. On the way to my meeting, I convinced myself that Terri's husband would listen to her. Julie's husband would take her out to dinner and not <u>make</u> her cook (my husband would never make me cook; remember, I already stated that I do it because I love it, but once you start to go down that road in your mind, rational thought goes out the door). By the time I got to that meeting, I had convinced myself that every husband in my world would have rolled out the red carpet for their spouses who asked them to take out the biscuits, while mine...well, let's just say that I wasn't thinking clearly.

I made it through the meeting. I headed back home, convinced that I would find Steve still glued to the television with the smoke alarm going off in the background (and he wouldn't notice), and I would have all kinds of ammunition for a great argument.

I walked up the steps, a little surprised not to see the fire trucks outside my house. I opened the front door, and the television was off. I entered the kitchen, and…

Steve had done the dishes, cleaned the kitchen, and left me a plate of beautifully cooked biscuits on the counter, with the soup ready for me to warm up.

I'm so grateful that only the Lord and I were privy to my thought bubble.

I found Steve (who was working on a house project that I wanted him to do), and I gave him a hug and a kiss…and a thank you for being the best husband I could have. Confused, he said, "You're welcome."

He's a smart man not to ask questions.

Don't let your mind go down the road of lust for something you don't have, when in fact it may be right in front of you.

LUST
CHARTERED FOR DESTRUCTION

If you are a child of the 60's, then surely you know the theme song to the television show about the seven passengers stranded on a desert island. If you are from that generation, then you also know that you can sing the song "Amazing Grace" to the tune of that theme song…but that's another story.

The premise of the television series was great. The trip was doomed before the curtain opens on the very first scene. In the intro song, passengers head out for a leisurely tourist trip, the weather turns, the ship is destroyed, and the unlucky seven are then stranded on a "deserted" island (that actually had more visitors on it than most churches do on any given Sunday). The story line centered around each attempt to get off the island and return home. What was scheduled to be merely a three-hour tour with the chartered boat turned into years and years of syndication for these castaways.

Had the millionaire and his wife on the show known that they were going to be stranded on that island for so long, they might have opted to take something more practical than buckets of money and trunks of minks. But, then, it's easy to say in hindsight, isn't it?

Rarely do we start something knowing and planning that it's going to be destroyed and that our best-laid plans will amount to nothing. And yet, every time we lust for something, we are chartering the boat of our lives that can only have one destination: destruction. But, like the members of the S.S. Minnow, we, too, seem to think we can take this ship somewhere else.

Lust is an attempt at an instant fix. People who seek an instant high find themselves chartering their own boat of life to destruction, since the most they can expect is a momentary satisfaction that, in the end, leaves them emptier than when they started.

The Samaritan woman found herself seeking one husband after another, because she never understood love. She didn't get what it could be like to find fulfillment in life. Her life had become about scratching the current itch. That is, until Jesus came along.

Think it's something only those in Jesus's day had to deal with? Think again.

Every day, we can watch others who choose poorly as they seek an instant fix and don't recognize the consequences that follow.

But remember: it's easier to see in others what we don't want to see in ourselves.

Lust destroys. It kills the essence of what God is trying to create in us. Whether we realize it or not, whenever we walk down the road of lust, we're walking down the road of danger, the road of risk, the road splattered with "Do Not Enter" signs. We are destined to suffer the consequences. And still, many of us choose to go down the road. We still lust for things we can't have. We go after things that satisfy a momentary desire instead of going to Christ, knowing that only in Him can we be completely satisfied.

The Samaritan woman found it, you know—true joy, real happiness, actual fulfillment—in Jesus. Her life changed immediately, because her heart changed immediately. Once she drew upon Living water, she understood the true high of tasting heaven.

I've seen people in a third-world country who will, without even thinking about it, drink from a creek filled with bacteria, instead of traveling to a well or finding purified water. The result is often sickness and even death. We do the same thing when we try to draw from the river of lust: we attempt to find momentary satisfaction, instead of drawing upon the living and purified water that satisfies our thirst and quenches our soul. The difference between those people drinking from the contaminated river and us drinking from the river of lust is this: they often don't have the choice.

You do.

Are you looking to charter a boat that will lead you down a pathway of doom, or will you let Jesus be your captain this day, as you surrender the ship of your life to Him?

LUST

MINE-MINE-MINE

It's that scene in "Finding Nemo" where the seagulls are sitting on the rocks in the water. They sound exactly like seagulls squawking, until the scene moves in, and you can hear what the seagulls are actually saying: "Mine, Mine, Mine, Mine, Mine…"

The pelican in front of the gulls has a crab he's trying to eat, and the seagulls are singularly focused on wanting that crab for themselves. Of course, in true Nemo fashion, the crab ends up escaping.

"Mine…mine…mine…"

The whole "mine" thing, now that's just funny.

I just can't figure out why.

I took a work trip to California. It was in August, when southern California is blistering hot. Now, whenever I have to go on a trip and rent a car, I try to get the best convertible possible (which was great for a trip like this, but is much less fun when the destination point is Minnesota in January. I'm just saying.).

On this particular southern California trip, I rented a luxury convertible. I <u>loved</u> it. The engine was powerful. There was enough room for me and my luggage (I've learned not to get the sporty convertibles, because I'm not a light packer). I could keep up with Los Angeles traffic in the evening (no joke—90 miles an hour, and I wasn't passing *anyone*). I drove wherever this little machine would take me. The driving around was probably the best part of the trip.

I could get used to this.

Then I came home.

The next week, I drove my old, dinged up SUV to work. My sad car—the first weekend after I had bought it, its side met the side of a 15-passenger van being driven by an elderly woman who had borrowed it "just once" from her son, and she didn't know that she was scraping the side of my car as she was trying to exit her space at the hospital. I was walking out of the hospital at the time and heard the horrendous sound of metal-on-metal and felt terrible for the poor schmuck that was getting sideswiped. A couple of years later, somebody ran into my car's left flank and then took off. It's a good enough car, and it runs just fine; it just doesn't look that great.

Okay, so back to me getting to work. You can imagine my surprise when I pulled my completely reliable if increasingly unattractive rig into the parking lot at work, and found my space…next to the *tan luxury convertible*—almost exactly the same car that I had just given up at the airport in LA.

I lusted after that car.

My first thought was: Could this be a wicked surprise from my husband, who had been hearing nothing but how great this car had been? Could I get my lust satisfied? But fairly quickly I was certain this was not my future car.

Then whose magic carpet ride does this belong to? Who will I direct my lust-quickly-turning-to-envy toward?

It turned out that the car's new owner is the woman who worked right next to me. I should tell you here that this woman is the most incredible, faith-filled woman—I learn from her, I laugh with her, and I love her like a sister. Or, maybe I should say a half-sister, since she's half my size and if I sat on her I would squish her like a bug.

But I wouldn't, because I adore her.

Anyway, she had just lost her mother, and it was her mother's car, so she inherited it.

My friend said it was comforting to be able to drive around in her mom's car, at least for a while.

Comforting? Yeah, it's comforting. It's got comforting heated leather seats that conform to the driver's body type, a comforting Bose stereo, comforting bells and whistles, and a comforting engine that will take you from zero to yikes in 4.2 seconds.

Now I was *drooling* with envy. I had transitioned from "I want this" to "I wish I had what she has."

Yes, I know: my envy could not have come at a more inappropriate time.

I mean, come on—it's not like her mom lent her the car.

Her mom just *died*.

And all I could think about was how lucky she was to get that car, and how in the world I'll ever be able to have a car like that.

I am humiliated, ashamed, and embarrassed as I write this.

I'm an imbecile for having thought that way.

But it's the truth, and if I'm ever going to learn, then it might as well be through the truth.

Okay, so what did I learn from this little experience? First: Lust makes me tunnel-visioned. Second: Envy clouds rational thought.

That's an understatement.

It's easy to see something that somebody else has that I want, but not see the whole picture. It's not difficult to get completely wrapped up, emotions and all, in something that is here today, and gone tomorrow.

I am learning.

Slowly.

I think I need to go call my mom and tell her I'm thankful to have her instead of a fancy car.

Of course, she won't understand.

But I will.

LUST
NOT SO PRIVATE

I get bugged when I start saying things to my kids that my mother used to say to me.

"If you can't say something nice, don't say anything at all."

"If you don't have time to do it right, when will you find the time to do it over?"

I really don't like those sayings.

Ever since we were little we were reading quotes that my mom cut out and taped to the refrigerator door, so we kids had no choice but to stare them down as we were reaching for a snack.

Unfortunately, her underhanded tactics worked. Now, when one of my kids is commanded to perform a dangerous and completely unfair task (like shovel out a bedroom) and they do the job half-way (at best), I find myself quoting one of those phrases.

"Now, Ben, if you don't have time to do it right, when will you find the time to do it over?"

It's typically only half out of my mouth before I realized I had become my mother.

How did they get into my head?

They probably got there because they ring true.

When we kids were teenagers and seeking the freedom that we most certainly deserved, and my parents felt the need to torture us with rules and curfews and such, they typically followed their unfair demands with this statement:

"Our house, our rules. When you are in your own home, you can make your own rules."

Oh, you'd better believe I'll make my own rules, Mother. There's no way anybody's going to make me do the dishes, or be home by 10 o'clock at night, or take out the trash. My life's gonna be great then!

I think many of us get on our own and learn fairly quickly that, if we don't take out the trash, then bad smells happen. If I don't get a good sleep at night, then bad work happens the next day. If I don't do the dishes, then I won't have any dishes.

Funny how that happens.

For some reason, we seem to think that sin in general, and lust in particular, is a private sin. We think that what we do doesn't affect other people. After all, lust is something that people only think about—it's internal—so how in the world could it affect anyone else?

Right?

The thing is, though, that lust does affect the community around you. If you're married, then lusting for somebody else affects a marriage. If you're single, you'll find that lust affects other relationships, as unmet wants take over the mind. Ultimately, when we lust for something—or someone—we are jumping out of God's plan and trying to jump into our own.

And we've all seen how that goes.

Isaiah 53:6:

We all, like sheep, have gone astray, each of us has turned to his own way; and the Lord has laid on him the iniquity of us all.

When we step outside the circle of God's desires for us, we affect those around us. We're not as covert as we like to think we are. Our poor choices affect our other relationships.

The Samaritan woman's actions affected others—think about the five husbands and the man she was living with. Consider her relationships with others in the community, too: how do you think they felt about her? Do you think any of the other women would trust her with their husbands?

See—sin is not private.

A man who lusts after a car he can't afford can make himself angry because he's not wealthy enough. A woman who longs to look prettier, or thinner, or pooched up here or toned down there, finds herself bitter and angry. Lust is internal, but it's like a poison that affects us from the inside out. Lust shoots right to the heart, and when we lust for things, we divide the heart--it's no longer fully devoted to what it was created for. To lust is to lose your love for God. You cannot lust and love at the same time. So, clearly, lust does affect us...and others.

God really wants us to be devoted to Him. When He has your whole heart, you can start to look at the world through God-colored glasses.

My mom taught me that.

Thanks, Mom.

LUST
THE SUBSTITUTE

My daughter was four years old at the time. I was picking her up from school, when she came out of her classroom sucking on a sickeningly-sweet peppermint-flavored lollipop. She had it all over her mouth and running down her chin when she looked up to me and said, "Look, Mom! I have a minty lollipop—now I won't have to brush my teeth tonight!"

She has somehow associated mint flavoring with fresh teeth and breath, and she assumed that the lollipop would be a sufficient substitute for the annoyance of brushing that evening.

She was wrong.

Kids look for substitutes all over the place, don't they? A jump in a pond should replace a bath? A green Jolly Rancher should replace a green bean?

But it's not just kids who try to do that. They're just usually more obvious. Grown ups seek substitutes in our lives all the time, too. Though we seem to search the world trying to find fulfillment in the world, there really is no substitute for what the Lord brings us, when we bring ourselves to Him.

Toothpaste helps scrub your teeth clean. What are you trying to use to scrub your heart clean?

LUST
BUMPER STICKERS

Bumper stickers can say a lot about a car's driver. In a few words, we in the car behind discover what's important to them; the sort of music they like to listen to; and the sorts of things they like to consume, inhale, read, and believe. We see where they've come from and where they're going, and often more than we may want to know as we're tailgating them (there are bumper stickers for that, too).

One of my least favorite bumper stickers, though, is this one:

He who dies with the most toys wins.

The problem? It encapsulates an attitude of *Buy this, consume that, surround yourself with as much stuff as you can. You really ARE able to have the things you lust for; what's more, it should be your life's goal.*

See how much is wrapped up in an 8-word bumper sticker?

When I see that bumper sticker, I typically think of this other one:

He who dies with the most toys...still dies.

It's that second quote that brings the first one back home.

Whatever you lust after is a momentary high. It truly is here today and gone tomorrow.

And you can't take it with you.

A friend always wanted a fancy car (the "friend" was not me, in case you're recalling that previous story). He spent nearly a year perusing too many car dealerships and too many websites looking for just that perfect convertible. The more he searched, the more his original idea of the "cute little two-seater for fun summer jaunts" grew to the "much more functional (and expensive) hard-top so I can use it all year." He went from looking for a 15-year-old convertible to casing new-car dealers.

Then came the September afternoon when he had chest pains and landed in the hospital.

The next week, a beautiful BMW convertible landed in his garage.

As he looks back now, he tells others, "I admit it. I got scared that I wasn't going to live much longer, so it was time to 'CARPE CAR (seize the car),' live for today, get it and enjoy it while I can."

But then it began to break down. And all of a sudden, this dream car wasn't as exciting to my friend as it had been. The idea of the wind rushing through his hair and the sun drenching his face became secondary to the responsibilities of car ownership.

What a great lesson to us me, which I keep learning, over and over Whether it's with a bicycle or a boat, a trip or a treadmill, when we want something so much that it takes over our thoughts, it probably isn't worth getting...or at least it becomes a great illustration to others.

There's nothing wrong with having some things that make life fun. The challenge is when having those things becomes the purpose of your life, rather than letting your relationship with The Lord take first place.

Rather than looking back at the end of my life and thinking about what I've ridden in, I'm now a little more focused on knowing where I'm going.

LUST
FOCUS

We see lust so often that we've become numb to it.

Why do you think hamburger chains use a scantily-clad woman washing a soaped up car to highlight their latest burger--because soap and bikinis say anything about an entree?

Of course not.

When you're watching a commercial, are you sometimes hard-pressed to figure out what the commercial is really advertising? The ad company wants you to lust after their product, but often they believe they need to grab you by tempting you to lust after something else, first.

Crazy.

And it works.

Be on the lookout for the subtle (and not-so-subtle) ways we are tempted by lust. Keep your eyes on the prize described in Philippians 3:13-15:

13 Brothers and sisters, I do not consider myself yet to have taken hold of it. But one thing I do: Forgetting what is behind and straining toward what is ahead, 14 I press on toward the goal to win the prize for which God has called me heavenward in Christ Jesus.

Don't get distracted.

LUST

GRAHAM CRACKERS AND LUST?

I was watching a cooking show, and the competitors were told to make a hopped-up version of S'Mores--you know, that triple combination of roasted marshmallow, chocolate, and graham cracker. During the baking, the host mentioned something about graham crackers originating from a minister who was trying to teach healthy living.

So I decided to look up the history of the graham cracker.

You're not gonna believe this.

The graham cracker came into existence in 1829 in Boundbrook, New Jersey. Its creator was a Presbyterian minister named Sylvester Graham (so far, I like this--having a Presbyterian invent something as wonderful as a graham cracker).

The graham cracker was designed to be a health food as part of the Graham Diet. Interesting is that the reverend's diet was not intended for weight loss or even weight management; his diet, consisting mostly of bland foods, was meant to suppress what he considered unhealthy carnal urges--what we would call lust. For some reason, Graham associated lust with flavorful foods. One of his many theories was that it was possible to curb the sexual appetite if only bland foods were ingested. Interestingly, another key figure on the American food scene who agreed with Graham was Dr. John Harvey Kellogg, who invented corn flakes cereal.

Graham crackers were typically made with what is now called graham flour--coarsely stone-ground whole wheat flour. These days, they are often made mainly of the refined, bleached white flour to which the Rev. Graham was opposed. Graham crackers are also not the bland snack they started out being, because now they are topped with cinnamon, sugar, chocolate...or a combination of these three. These days, graham crackers could hardly be considered a health food.

Eat bland foods, and you won't lust. It's an interesting concept, but one that has never been proven. Easier might be to stay away from temptation, to pray that The Lord might take this burden, and to live your life in a way that is honoring to God ...no matter how bland or flavorful your food is.

The next time you grab a graham cracker, realize there's a story behind it--just like you have a story behind your actions.

And don't forget to enjoy--and appreciate--every bite.

CHAPTER FIVE: ANGER—DON'T GET MAD AT WHAT YOU'RE ABOUT TO READ

ANGER
DON'T GET MAD AT WHAT
YOU'RE ABOUT TO READ

Matthew 5:21-26, Jesus Turns the Tables

21"You have heard that it was said to the people long ago, 'Do not murder, and anyone who murders will be subject to judgment.' 22But I tell you that anyone who is angry with his brother will be subject to judgment. Again, anyone who says to his brother, 'Raca,' is answerable to the Sanhedrin. But anyone who says, 'You fool!' will be in danger of the fire of hell.

23"Therefore, if you are offering your gift at the altar and there remember that your brother has something against you, 24leave your gift there in front of the altar. First go and be reconciled to your brother; then come and offer your gift.

25"Settle matters quickly with your adversary who is taking you to court. Do it while you are still with him on the way, or he may hand you over to the judge, and the judge may hand you over to the officer, and you may be thrown into prison. 26I tell you the truth, you will not get out until you have paid the last penny.

Black and white. It seems that there used to be a chasm between good and bad, with the majority of us falling into the category of "good." The only real danger in "these parts" were the bad guys, with their black hats and waxed, pencil-thin mustaches (and bad-guy background music), who were eventually run out of town by the good guys (who came to save the day in, of course, their white hats).

Bad people were the pillagers of society, the mayhem-causers. The rest of us were in need of protection from them.

And then Jesus turns the tables on us...and narrows the chasm. He says that "<u>anyone</u> who is angry with his brother will be subject to judgment."

Anyone?

Seriously, Jesus, anyone??

That doesn't even make sense to my rational mind. After all, anger is not a defect in who we are; it's part of who we are. In fact, anger is a completely normal, often healthy, human emotion.

It's also one of the deadliest of the Deadlies, because of the way that we conceive of and deal with anger. We mostly misunderstand anger... and that's where the problem lies.

You know what anger is. You've felt it before—probably not so long ago. Sometimes it comes as a fleeting annoyance; other times it comes out as full rage.

Take a look at the other sins. Take pride. We don't misunderstand what that word means and how it applies to our lives. The same is true with envy and gluttony; we get them. We don't like them, but we get them.

But when it comes to anger, we waffle.

Ever heard someone justify their anger by using Jesus as an example? "Even Jesus got angry, when he turned the tables in the temple. You think that's not anger? Well, if Jesus can do it, and He never sinned, then I know that anger isn't a sin. So there!"

It's true. Jesus didn't sin. And He did get angry.

So...?

The problem rests in what we do with it.

Henry Fairlie describes the Deadly Sin of anger as "a disorderly outburst of emotion connected with the inordinate desire for revenge... it may be inordinate either in regard to the object on which it is vented, or in the degree in which it is fostered or expressed."

In the near future, you will more than likely come upon an opportunity for anger to arise. Maybe it will come when something falls on your foot, or when someone cuts you off on the highway. It may come in an act of injustice that you witness or that someone you love is experiencing. It might come when you are threatened by your environment or by the words that another person says. Perhaps it will appear when you--or someone else--questions your worth.

Typically, anger arises when we aren't expecting it. We could be feeling pretty good one moment, and then move into a fit of rage the next, because of what one person says, or as a result of hearing bad news. And that's when you feel it: the adrenaline rush of anger.

If you're worried that you might be stretching your toes across the line from sinless anger to deadly sin, then go back to that description from Henry Fairlie:

"A disorderly outburst of emotion connected with the inordinate desire for revenge...it may be inordinate either in regard to the object on which it is vented, or in the degree in which it is fostered or expressed."

Do you have that feeling that your ears are burning (that's the physical thing that happens to me--it may be different for you), coupled with a deep need to get back at that person, that thing, that injustice?

Remember: these sins become deadly when they are focused on self-righteousness. What's making you get so upset? What's getting you hot under the collar (or sweaty behind your knees)? If you can press your personal pause button and figure out whether or not your emotion is appropriate, and whether or not you feel the need for revenge, then you'll have a better chance of steering clear of this Deadly.

Have you ever heard the phrase, "There, but for the grace of God, go I"? These days, this saying is often used without the actual belief in the Christian God's control of all things and is used by believers and nonbelievers alike. It is suggested to have been coined in a seemingly more pious and devout era. The story that is widely circulated is that the phrase was first spoken by the English evangelical preacher and martyr, John Bradford (circa 1510–1555). He is said to have uttered the variant of the expression - "There, but for the grace of God, goes John Bradford," when seeing criminals being led to the scaffold. He didn't enjoy that grace for long, however. In 1555, he was burned at the stake. How positive would you be if you were walking toward your death? By all accounts, Bradford remained optimistic about his fate and is said to have suggested to a fellow victim that "we shall have a merry supper with the Lord this night."

There's an example of not letting anger get the best of you.

May you yield your feelings—not just the easy ones, but even the blood-boiling ones—to God, so that you truly might, as Paul declares, "be transformed by the renewing of your mind. Then you will be able to test and approve what God's will is—his good, pleasing, and perfect will" (Romans 12:2b).

ANGER

ALL ABOUT ME

Obedience plays a major role in this whole discipleship thing.

Let me just tell you right now how much I don't like obedience, mostly because it deals with the issue of control, which I do like.

Control is my friend. Obedience? Not so much.

For a number of years, a group of friends gathered each summer for a sailing trip. Each year, we rented a sailboat and sailed around the San Juan Islands in the Pacific Northwest. Stories abounded while we were on the high seas, but most of our adventures had to do with food rather than wind or water, as we never got our sailboat to go any faster than seven knots (which is 8 miles an hour to you landlubbers). We never really ran the risk of reenacting "A Perfect Storm"—our trips were more like a floating version of "Top Chef."

One of my friends—we'll call him Skipper Bob—is a well-trained sailor, and he was able to teach us actual sailing technique as we prepared for our trips each year (mostly so we'd be able to tell our stories with some degree of authenticity. Ahoy.).

We were about two days in on our first trip, when Skipper Bob gave me an offer I couldn't refuse: "Care to take the wheel for a while?"

I'd been waiting for my chance.

Now, this was no little raft—it was a 42-foot sailboat with three state rooms (that means three sleeping areas). So, once we monkeyed around with the sails for awhile, we headed south, right in the middle of Puget Sound, just west of the Seattle skyline.

Meanwhile, Skipper Bob took a comfortable seat right in the bow—that's the front—on a tiny triangular platform, with his legs hanging over so he could catch some waves.

He looked so comfortable with me confidently at the helm.

And life was great.

The wind then changed a bit, and I had to work harder to keep the boat pointed in the right direction. The more I turned the wheel, the more we began to tip…and tip…and tip. I started getting anxious, looking around me for assistance from the crew, but I couldn't see anyone around me. They were all sleeping and soaking up the sun, all except for Bob, who was having a great time kicking at the waves. It was then I realized that if all that tipping was a problem, then Bob would be back at the wheel in a heartbeat.

Once I managed my anxiety, I felt surprisingly in control, using the wind to fill the sails and guide the boat. I started feeling really confident about myself and my ability as a sailor…right up until the time that Skipper Bob returned, and I handed over the wheel to him…

…and he took the boat off of auto-pilot.

See, I was steering, I was in control to a degree, but I was never going to get us too off-track, because I was not ultimately in charge.

Now, let me stop here and just say this: If I had been Bob, I would have found this little display *hilarious.* I would have quietly tip-toed around to the other passengers and let them in on the secret that "Laurie isn't actually steering the boat—it's on <u>auto-pilot</u>! But shhhh, don't act like you know anything. Let's just watch."

Come to think of it, everybody did gather around pretty quickly after I recognized what had happened.

On the "Bob" end of this whole event, the situation is a riot.

On the "Laurie" end, however, it's a little less funny.

In fact, inside, my guts were burning. I didn't look like the master and commander. I didn't actually have control.

Most importantly, somebody else knew it.

The sin of anger can be found wherever I think I'm in control but then learn that I'm not…and somebody else is. When I am put in my place, and I think my place is loftier than it actually is. When I don't look as good as I'd like to look in any particular situation.

And the silly thing is that, typically, my response to that situation confirms the fact that I am exactly where I should be. If I mope (not that I ever mope), then that would prove I'm not the leader I claim to be. If I yell, then that would assure others that they don't have someone level-headed at the helm.

I did have another choice as I stood staring at the wheel: see this whole situation, not as an affront to me, but as something very funny. I could recognize that Bob did this to me for a reason; he could have tried it on anybody, but he figured that I would handle it well, or I would give the best response…or he actually wasn't sure that I would be able to handle the boat and wanted to keep us safe, but didn't want to hurt my feelings.

That last one is what a true leader does: leads with love. If I were wearing the captain shoes, would I have done it any differently?

ANGER

95 THESES

I teach Reformed History and Theology in the church (and sometimes even at the hospital where I work). So, a number of years ago, when our congregation was preparing to celebrate its 125th anniversary, I appreciated hearing the pastor share some of the historical highlights in both our specific church and the larger Christian church.

The week before the anniversary celebration, our pastor told the story of Martin Luther pounding his list of 95 Theses onto the Wittenberg Church Door in Germany. These 95 Theses, or arguments against mostly clerical abuses within the church, were a primary impetus for the Protestant Reformation. I've taught this dozens of times. I know the story. So it's not a story that surprises me. The pastor went on, assuring the congregation that, while this picture may seem a little out of the ordinary, we should recall that, in Martin Luther's day, the church door was more like a bulletin board, so pounding an article such as this wouldn't have been as outlandish as it might seem today. Besides, Martin Luther was angry. He didn't want to leave his post as a priest in his beloved church. He just wanted to focus back on Scripture, back on what mattered, back on Christ.

I looked over and found my 10-year-old, Mary Jo, taking notes. Not drawing, not making out a list of things she wanted to do later in the day, but taking notes.

I was so proud.

After church let out, she and I were walking hand-in-hand through the parking lot toward the car. I happened to glance down to see her looking all around in an effort to make sure that nobody else could hear us. Once we were out of earshot of any eavesdropping churchgoers, she stopped us and looked up.

Here's how the conversation went:

Mary Jo: "Okay, Mom, I have a question."

Mom: "Shoot."

Mary Jo: "So, let me get this right. There's this priest, and he doesn't like what's going on in the church. People aren't following the Bible. So this Martin Luther dude decides to do something that people will notice. He goes up to that church door, and he takes his hammer, and he pounds those ninety-five…you know…"

Mom: "Theses."

Mary Jo: "Uh, yeah."

Momentary pause, followed by…

Mary Jo: "I get that it was the common thing to do during his day, but did Martin Luther really nail ninety-five pieces of poop onto a church door?"

It took me a moment. Then I got it.

Mom: "Mare, look at my mouth. THESES, not FECES. Theses are statements. Feces, well, that's poop."

Another momentary paused, followed by…

Mary Jo: "Now THAT makes a lot more sense!"

I'll never be able to tell the history of the Reformation without talking about Martin Luther's 95 Feces. But I can't stop sharing the story of Martin Luther, because his is an example of the right sort of anger: a righteous anger, not a self-righteous one. He wanted to stay in his church. He wanted the reform to happen from within, not from without. But the church leaders wouldn't have any of that reform. That's because the things that Luther was arguing against were the very things that brought in the money and made for a better life for the priest of the day.

Perhaps Mary Jo's visual of what she thought Martin Luther had done wasn't so far off.

I wish I could be as angry about the right things (like what Martin Luther got set off about), and less upset about the things that don't matter.

What are you willing to pound to the door?

ANGER
THE BURN OF ANGER

My office was beginning to look—and feel—like my own personal sanctuary. I was ready to study this subject called ANGER. All that was lacking was a nice candle giving off a peaceful scent. So, I pulled a candle off the shelf and found a box of wooden matches I hadn't opened yet.

"Just one swipe of the match, and my sanctuary will be complete," I thought to myself.

I took that swipe, ready to light my candle...and the burning tip of the match flew off the wooden stick and landed just below my collarbone. The smell of burning flesh filled the air.

The scream was heard through my office door, past the outer office, and into the hallway. Immediately, a co-worker came running in to see if I was okay.

Did I thank him?

No.

Did I assure him I was okay?

Of course not.

Did I get angry at him?

You'd better believe it!

How DARE he actually come check on me, even though my scream warranted it. The gall!

What's more, I had to walk out of my office, my hand over my burn, looking for an ice pack. How humiliating. How dare everyone in the office (why were there so many people around, anyway?) be concerned?

My ears started to burn in anger.

Like gasoline on a fire, anger enflames the other sins. Anger is to an emotion as italics are to words: both emphasize what is already there. That's because we're often angry about the wrong things. And, when we're angry about the "right" things, we respond in the wrong ways, looking not to the Lord but to what's really important to me: me.

You know it: flames lick and leap where they have something to burn. And when any of the other Deadlies is around, anger is the fuel that makes that fire burn fiercest.

Anger is a Deadly Sin because it feeds and it breeds. It feeds on unrighteousness. It breeds judgment. And it is such a Deadly Sin because it wasn't created to be a sin at all, and it doesn't need to be.

We're reminded in the Psalms, and again in Ephesians, to not sin in our anger. It really is possible to be angry and not sin. One can also turn to the time when Jesus became angry with the people selling their wares in the temple and say that, since Jesus didn't sin, and He did become angry, then anger, therefore, isn't necessarily a sin.

That's true.

But what's also true is that we rarely become angry without sin. Want to figure out if you have the right kind of anger or the sinful sort of anger? Then ask yourself why you're angry. Your answer may tell you a lot.

That man cut you off at the stoplight. Three blocks later, you're still mad. Why?

Sinless or sinful anger?

Your life isn't going as you expected or wanted. And you're angry. Why?

Sinless or sinful anger?

Somebody is doing something you don't think they should get away with doing. You're hot under the collar. Why?

Sinless or sinful anger?

...Or did your match break apart and you're getting charred?

The truth is this: very rarely do we get angry without becoming self-centered. Maybe my anger comes about because of pride, or envy, or lust, because life isn't fair—and it never seems to be unfair to MY benefit. And the pot of anger begins to boil in my belly. And my heart begins to divide.

As you look at anger in your own life, look at it through the lens of Philippians 2:5, where Paul reminds us, "Let the same mind be in you that was in Christ Jesus." Are you angry about wrong things: your things, or about right things: God's things?

What would sinless anger really look like in your life today?

And how would you respond to it in a way that uplifts the Lord and doesn't cause you to hide from Him?

Let Jesus spark you.

ANGER
LET'S KILL 'EM!

Surely you've either been on a team or been a spectator watching…and you've gotten a little too into the game. Pretty soon, you're hearing the words, and you don't even realize that it's coming out of your mouth.

Let's Kill 'Em!

You just want to win the game. You don't really want to kill the other team—well, at least not literally.

That's where you've turned a corner in your attitude. It's no longer about your team just doing its best; it's about doing better than the other team. In fact, the only thing more satisfying than winning…is annihilating your opponent.

Games are meant to be about healthy and fun competition. But the pee-wee soccer match far too often turns into a gladiator fight to the death. Add to the mayhem an incorrect call by an umpire, and now an injustice must be righted. Fairness turns into revenge, and friends turn into enemies, when it all should have culminated in a team trip for an ice cream cone.

In Ephesians 4, Paul reminds us, "Don't let the sun go down on your anger, and do not give the devil a foothold." Instead, reconcile--make up--with one another with a heart of love, and see people not as enemies but as gifts from God. If we can look at others (that includes parents of an opposing soccer team…or the umpire of that baseball team…or the coach that didn't play your star player) as children of and gifts from God, we can turn that anger and vengeance to love.

Imagine if God threw around His anger the way we do.

I, for one, am really thankful He doesn't.

Instead of crying out, "That's not fair," Jesus cries out, "Father, forgive them."

May we learn to take on Christ's heart and attitude toward those around us.

Even when we're around the other team.

ANGER
HIDING IT

"I'm fine."

Don't you love hearing those words through clenched teeth?

Clearly, the person speaking is anything but fine.

Some people actually believe that just because they don't punch a wall or say mean things in front of a person, they can convince the world they really aren't angry. In fact, because I don't yell out in my car or scream or cry out loud at the injustices around me, I might see myself as more holy than those who actually do those things.

Similarly, the person who is saccharin-sweet during the day and then goes home that night and gossips or is judgmental about everyone they crossed paths with is doing more than damaging their reputation; they're damaging themselves. Emotional tensions have physical manifestations. So, if it's not enough to just be thinking about your reputation, think about what being angry and bitter does to the body...your physical body, and the collective body of those around you.

These are just some of the consequences of the deadly sin of anger. And they are just as painful, harmful, and long-lasting as putting a fist through a wall might be. In fact, they may be even more so.

In Matthew 5:22b, Jesus says, "Anyone who says to his brother, 'Raca,' is answerable to the Sanhedrin. But anyone who says, 'You fool!' will be in danger of the fire of hell." The word 'Raca' is the word the people in Jesus's day used when they wanted to call someone empty-headed. It's quite demeaning. According to Jewish custom, the person who speaks against another brother is subject to the consequences imposed by the Sanhedrin, the highest court and council of the ancient Jewish nation. It's a pretty big deal. But then, Jesus takes it another step. He tells the people that anyone who says someone else is foolish better be careful, because the person who speaks those words will not be judged by the Sanhedrin but by God Himself on the day of Judgment.

Those secret sins do more damage to the body of Christ--the church--more than nearly anything else. They destroy its infrastructure.

And it's the main reason why those outside the church want nothing to do with "those Christians."

I hear it all the time.

"They're hypocrites."

"They act like they're better than everyone else."

"They are all high and mighty on Sunday and then gossips and cheats on Monday."

God wants His followers to "go into the world and make disciples of all nations." But we followers can be the greatest detriment to nonbelievers.

We have a real opportunity to be clear: I am a Christian, not because I'm better than anyone else, but because I recognize that I am the greatest of sinners. I am a hypocrite, and that's why I need The Lord. I have no right to pretend I'm better than anyone else, or that I'm "fine," when the only reason I am living and breathing is because of God's grace.

I have no right to be angry and bitter and act like I'm not.

How about you?

ANGER

MANAGE THIS!

In 1999, a movie came out about a mob boss needing psychotherapy. The tagline for the movie was this:

"New York's most powerful gangster is about to get in touch with his feelings. YOU try telling him his 50 minutes are up."

The gangster was named Paul Vitti, who was being counseled by Dr. Ben Sobel. They spend the movie trying to work through Vitti's anger issues.

In one scene, Dr. Sobel is trying to get Vitti to calm down. The doctor thinks that if he can teach Vitti new ways to manage his anger, then he just might stop shooting people (and his anxiety attacks might subside to boot). Dr. Sobel tells Vitti, "You can't keep doing this. You want to get physical? Take a walk. Get a punching bag. Hit a pillow."

At that, Vitti takes out a .9 mm and shoots the daylights out of a pillow.

In shock, Dr. Sobel asks, "Feel better now?"

Vitti replies, "Yeah, I do."

I love that scene. It's outlandish. It's hilarious. And at times, it's exactly how I would love to respond. Unfortunately, it's not really a responsible way to manage anger. Punching a wall, screaming into a pillow, shooting a decorator cushion--anytime you "lose it," you're showing that you aren't "managing it."

And the only way to manage your anger is to reconcile whatever the issue is, whether it's with another person or with The Lord.

In verses 23 and 24 of Matthew 5, Jesus says, "Therefore, if you are offering your gift at the altar and there remember that your brother has something against you, leave your gift there in front of the altar. First go and be reconciled to your brother; then come and offer your gift." Jesus is giving us a constructive solution for dealing with our anger—and getting our hearts and minds right, both with each other and with The Lord.

When we choose not to reconcile with another, we're saying that we'll manage it our way.

I'll deal with it the way I want to, thank you very much.

When we do that, we're not getting rid of anger, we're just spreading it around and taking it out on a someone or something innocent (oh, if some pillows could talk!).

But remember, reconciliation means confronting someone in brotherly love. Reconciliation calls us to respond to each other with a heart of Christ, not a heart of vengeance or an attempt to prove who is right and who is wrong.

How do you manage your anger? Do you shoot pillows, or do you shoot looks? Do you gossip? Is there judgment in your heart? Or are you able to go to your brother or sister and share your hurts and pains as you reconcile with each other, so instead of throwing punches you are throwing each other a life line?

ANGER
FIGHT...OR FLIGHT?

A common topic in my healthcare world is insurance. Usually, the conversation quickly moves to its cost, because it keeps heading one way: up. I get to hear it from the angles of the patient and of the physician, because both are frustrated that a big reason the cost is astronomical is because of all those frivolous lawsuits. You can sue for anything these days, from spilled coffee to spoiled plans. I looked on the internet to read about all kinds of frivolous lawsuits, which range from the ridiculous to the "I can't believe they even thought of that." Typically, these lawsuits seem to find their foundation in blame. "It's not my fault, but it's someone's, and I'm going to make them pay." There's a sense of self-righteousness, of vengeance, of taking the bull by the horns...of anger run amok.

Then there's the flip-side: some people choose to be doormats, as they run from any opposition, any confrontation, any disagreement, all the while getting eaten up inside.

God doesn't direct us to fight for revenge...or to be doormats. We have been created by the King of Kings and Lord of Lords. That allows us to be assertive in who we are, but not aggressive and a steamroller with our attitudes. We're supposed to use our frustration appropriately, and fight against injustice in the world, not fight to get things we don't deserve.

We have opportunities to make anger an ally. But we need to recognize that we have ample opportunities before us without making up frivolous ones. How many of us are taking our anger for injustice and helping to feed a child in need? How about running--or walking--a marathon in a friend or family member's name to raise money to find a cure for cancer? How about going down to the local jail to volunteer in creative ways? That's taking action from anger and making anger an ally.

We can choose something other that flight or flight. We can actually allow the Jesus desire within us to change the world around us, as we use the same anger that God has instilled in us to really make a difference.

One day, Jesus walked into the temple. There were merchants taking sections of the temple meant to be used for the Gentiles to worship. Most Jews didn't respect the Gentiles, and they saw the temple as a place for their own purposes. But Jesus saw things differently. He began to turn the tables on them. Jesus took action from the injustice He saw: the Gentiles didn't have a place to worship God, and the sellers took over that space and turned it into a market.

Anger can be righteous. We don't have to run from it or fight so we can prove we're right. We do, however, have a responsibility as Christians to stand up for injustice and allow the Lord to transform society as we know it today, as we speak out, not with a spirit of vengeance or timidity, but with one of humility and love.

Out of that love, Jesus turned the tables and opened the door for the Gentiles to worship.

What tables can you turn today?

CHAPTER SIX: GREED—HOW MUCH IS TOO MUCH?

GREED
HOW MUCH IS TOO MUCH?

Luke 12:13-21, The Parable of the Rich Fool

> *13Someone in the crowd said to him, "Teacher, tell my brother to divide the inheritance with me."*

> *14Jesus replied, "Man, who appointed me a judge or an arbiter between you?" 15Then he said to them, "Watch out! Be on your guard against all kinds of greed; a man's life does not consist in the abundance of his possessions."*

> *16And he told them this parable: "The ground of a certain rich man produced a good crop. 17He thought to himself, 'What shall I do? I have no place to store my crops.'*

> *18"Then he said, 'This is what I'll do. I will tear down my barns and build bigger ones, and there I will store all my grain and my goods. 19And I'll say to myself, "You have plenty of good things laid up for many years. Take life easy; eat, drink and be merry." '*

> *20"But God said to him, 'You fool! This very night your life will be demanded from you. Then who will get what you have prepared for yourself?'*

> *21"This is how it will be with anyone who stores up things for himself but is not rich toward God."*

Most of us don't call it avarice; we call it greed. But greed seems to trigger images mainly of money. Avarice is one of those "big" words that's a little vague...and even sounds more sinful than greed.

The word "avarice" is closely related to the word "covetousness." To have avarice is to covet. It's the desire to have something or someone. It's the obsession for amassing things material, ignoring the tuggings of the heart. It is cupidity—an overwhelming craving to have more than one needs. In the end, perhaps it can be defined this way: it is greed… to the nth degree.

Think of Scrooge from "A Christmas Carol." Here's a man who held his fortune so tightly in his grip that the imprints from the coins would stain his sweaty palms. This man had so much but would lend nothing. He squeezed more and more than what he needed out of those who had less and less of what they needed. Avarice is found in the one who holds onto his wealth and who is driven to grasp for more—usually at the expense, and always without the consideration, of others.

In The Seven Deadly Sins Today, Henry Fairlie writes, "One who is avarice is one whose appetites are stimulated so that the product to be consumed is more for the sake of possessing than it is for using. Avarice is the love of possessing; that possession is more important than the love of the possession itself."

That quote makes me take a material inventory. How many coffee pots, shoes, pens, shoes, articles of clothing, tools, shoes, and pieces of sporting equipment does one person need? Perhaps you could claim some form of greed. It's not that you need five or six fishing rods. It's not that I need seven pair of pink shoes (although we women know that none of those shoes is actually pink; there's the fuchsia flat, the rose slide, the blush stiletto, the flesh loafer…well, anyway, you get the point). It's not that you need a piece of jewelry for every outfit or a pen for every day of the week. But it's not difficult to start to slide into thinking that we do need something and then justify that need. Let's face it: most of us spend a fair amount of time looking for, and getting, what we want more often than what we need.

Planning for the future is one thing. Continuing to pack away for that possible rainy day, not only during the drought, but even during the flood--that's when it's time to consider that greed may be an issue. Ask yourself this: are you being a good steward of the resources God is giving you, or are you trying to take control to such a degree that you no longer depend on The Lord?

Friends were celebrating their 60th wedding anniversary, and the whole family came to the house to celebrate. Even with this large Italian family in attendance, loads of cake were left over. I went to the basement pantry to get a new roll of foil to wrap the cake in so it could be frozen and they could chomp on the dessert for years to come. When I opened the pantry door and looked up onto the shelves, I found the foil.

Twenty-three rolls of it.

The husband had been saving the foil for a rainy day. Whenever it was on sale, he stocked up. The problem was that he had bought it so long ago that now, instead of having 23 rolls of foil available, there were 23 rusted, solid tubes of former foil in boxes. It was useless. He had worked so hard to be prepared in the event of a foil-tastrophe, but his best laid plans fell short. I learned later that items like these were extremely hard to come by during The Great Depression, and this couple didn't want to live through that again. It made complete sense why they had 23 rolls of foil. But it helped me look at myself and the things that I collect.

We have so many resources in our country. We are an affluent nation. According to one internet article on Greed, there are hundreds of billionaires in the United States alone. We are back to the kind of extravagant living the likes of which has not been seen in over a century. Julian Edney, the author of the article, went on to say the following:

"By historical accounts this is a nation of persistent and resilient people with an unshakable mission: the pursuit of happiness. This idea of happiness is largely connected with wealth (and this connection has long philosophic roots)."

Sure, not everyone can be a billionaire. Still, many are living quite affluent lives. And yet, there are millions and millions who go through each day wondering if they will have enough food to make it until tomorrow.

When it comes to greed, it's easy for me to simply say, "Hey, I work hard for my money, I work hard for my things, and those other people can—and should—do the same."

If that's you, then don't get too comfortable. Doesn't Jesus speak on that in the parable in Luke 12, as the rich man builds his storehouses so he can eat, drink, and be merry down the road? If we're not careful, we can find that greed is the slippery slope on which we can slide into the other sin of sloth, becoming spiritually lazy, as we no longer need to rely on God, since we can go out and buy everything we want ourselves.

Christ calls us to something that greed can't buy: dependence. He doesn't call us to be financially poor, but poor in spirit, which means we need to come to realize that the things we have are not our own; they belong to God. They are not to be hoarded, buried, or treasured. They are just things—things that can quickly come and quickly go. We can be thankful for what we have, and we can share from every part of it... not only from our abundance.

Where are your treasures? Are you holding stock in things that decay, or holding onto the truth of God?

Your answer may make all the difference.

GREED
YOUR LIFE MUST BE DIFFICULT

Many of my friends have been to Haiti. It started with a couple I knew. Their passion led to an eventual ministry, which grew into a relationship, and now an unlikely group of Americans and Haitians are inextricably bound together.

I mentioned earlier that I "delivered" a baby while in Haiti. But that wasn't the thing that stands out most in my mind from my adventures on the island of Hispaniola (Haiti inhabits the western third the island, and the Dominican Republic takes up the eastern two-thirds).

My time in Haiti was spent with a medical team that drove from Port-au-Prince to the tiny village of Terre Blanche, 170 kilometers on sometimes paved roads, through often dangerous territory, and around the most impoverished and desolate land and kindest people I've ever encountered. We set up shop in the village church, and from Monday through Friday we were a makeshift clinic/hospital that saw 1500 Haitians walk, limp, and be carried through the doors. The Haitian Methodist Minister that organizes the regular immigration of American medical teams has a system for prioritizing who enters at what time. He requires some sort of participation on the part of the Haitians, typically a few dollars, but for the money given the one coming to the clinic receives whatever medical care and medicine needed, plus enough rice and beans to more than cover the amount paid. This system has helped the area Haitians become more responsible and learn how to plan and care for themselves and those around them. While the medical team is doing what they do, another team provides a Vacation Bible School program of sorts for the area children; as many as 300 kids gather every day to sing, to learn about the love The Lord has for them, and to enjoy such frivolities as coloring with actual crayons.

It is a completely different world.

On this particular trip, my task was to pray for and with each person that came into the clinic, to count out pills and place them in baggies, and to help with the children's program. The days were long, the air was hot (we were in Haiti in August, when the thick, 110-degree, wet air would become nearly unbearable, when all of a sudden in the middle of the day a torrential downpour would clean the entire environment, and then the air would begin to build up again), and we tired easily. By evening each day, we were all exhausted and went to sleep long before the sun went down.

Several healthy Haitians were hired to assist in the clinic each trip. All would travel, typically by foot or on Tap-Tap (old run-down open-air trucks that were piled high with locals holding on for dear life as they travelled from one part of town or one community to another). During our break in the mid-afternoon each day (during the downpours), we had opportunity to talk with these locals. Since I am fluent in French, I had the privilege of long conversations with numerous Haitians (while Creole is the native language, a Haitian with any education would learn French).

It was one delightful young Haitian man that stands out to me in particular.

I can't remember his name, but I will never forget the conversation.

We spoke about things in general at first: where he was born, a little about his family, a touch about things he was good at (he liked to work with tools). He said he was from Gonaives, which is about 10 miles from the village we were working in. Since he couldn't afford transportation, he walked to Terre Blanche each morning on the "road" (which is more like millions of potholes put together in a path through the rocky landscape). He didn't really have a home anymore, but he always found a place to sleep at night. What he owned was mostly what he carried with him. He hoped to become a handyman someday, "The Lord willing," he said.

His smile seemed so out of place to me.

But it was his next words that have haunted me ever since. He looked at me with care in his eyes, and he said in French, "Pastor Laurie, your life must be so difficult at home."

I figured I had misunderstood his French. Maybe I didn't interpret his words correctly. Our conversation had taken a sudden turn, and I wasn't certain that I heard right.

I looked at him, pointed to myself, and, again in French, asked, "My life? Did you say that my life must be tough?" I used slightly different words so that I would be sure that I was understanding.

"Yes, your life."

I was stunned. Didn't this fellow just tell me he had no home, he had no things, he had no money, he had nothing? And my life is difficult? I tried to regroup as (in as calm a manner I could muster) I asked, "How do you figure that?"

He replied, "Pastor Laurie, I have no home to be concerned about. I have no job to get to, other than this. My only worry for today is where I'm going to find a meal this evening. But you--you have property to keep, you have a job with many responsibilities, you have bills to pay, you have things to manage, you have people that depend on you, you have material goods to keep track of...your life must be so difficult."

That evening, I couldn't get my exhausted body to sleep. The all-night guards walked the perimeter of our village to keep us safe from the looters. The rhythm of the drums that the witch doctors played outside the camp (to keep us awake--we were taking away their livelihood by being there and helping people learn about the Lord instead of voodoo) made for great background noise. I kept staring up at the ceiling of the pup tent I was sharing with another nurse, and all I could think was, "I have everything I need...and then some. How could my life be tougher than his?"

In the end, I learned he was right. Sure, his concerns were the biggies: food and shelter. But my worries were many, and most of them centered around the stuff I had accumulated. I live in a nice home, with lots of land. I have to pay for the stuff to keep my home and my land in working condition. I pay for my phone and my cell phone and my internet and my appliances and the electricity to keep my appliances going and the repair man for when they don't keep going. I pay for my car and its gas and upkeep and license tabs and my license and my... and my...

And my, oh, my, I get it.

My stuff has changed my life. And often not for the better.

Wanting control is a form of greed. I want to surround myself with everything so I don't ever have to ask for anything.

And then I don't need God anymore, because I'm in charge.

Right up until I'm not.

Have you let your life revolve around your stuff, or are you free? What do you worry about?

The answer will tell you how difficult your life really is...and how easy it could be.

GREED
A Long Way to Go

Surely you've heard this joke:

A rich man who was very near death was upset because he had worked hard for his money and he wanted to take it with him to heaven. So be began to pray that he might be able to take some of his wealth with him.

An angel appeared and informed the man that God had decided to allow him to take one suitcase to heaven. Overjoyed, the man gathered his largest suitcase, filled it with pure gold bars, and placed it beside his bed. The man soon died and showed up at the Gates of Heaven to greet St. Peter. Seeing the suitcase, St. Peter said, "Hold on, you can't bring that in here!"

The man quickly explained to St. Peter that he had been given permission, and he suggested that St. Peter verify his story with the Lord. So Peter did. Sure enough, the man was correct. Peter returned and declared, "You're right. You are allowed one bag, but I'm supposed to check its contents before letting you through."

St. Peter opened the suitcase to inspect what the man found to be too precious to leave behind. Staring into the suitcase, Peter shook his head and turned to the man. With a curious look on his face, St. Peter exclaimed to the man, "You brought pavement?!"

How much stuff am I holding on to that I really don't need--and really don't use?

When we bought a car a few years ago, we decided that we would clear out the garage so the car would always be able to fit into it. So the four of us--the two grown-ups, and the two indentured servants...er, I mean kids (they just acted as if they were indentured servants during this particular task)--set to work to clean up the garage. We moved the four-wheeler to one end; the snow-blower to another; all the fishing gear to the side; the sprinkler parts to a shelf; the extra refrigerator and the extra freezer to an easily accessible area; the 8 coolers, stacked neatly, under the ladder that leads to the attic; the two giant, rolling toolboxes next to the shop table; the two shop-vacs next to the toolboxes; the shelf unit that holds all the extra kitchen supplies near the fridge; the canning supplies next to the shelf; and so on. After several hours, the garage was looking pretty good, so I moved the car into the garage, and life was grand.

Until we bought another car...and started arguing about which car gets to be in the garage.

And then my parents came over for dinner one night, and my dad heard me make some snippy comment about not having any room in the garage. Gently, and quietly, he commented, "I think your garage is bigger than ours, and we put both of our cars in the garage."

That's when it finally hit me that we have all kinds of stuff in the garage, and very little of it needs to be there. Most of it, in fact, is extra stuff that we have no business keeping on hand.

And now we fit both cars side-by-side. Sure, in order to get out of the car you have to open the door slightly, squeeze yourself through the hole like a sausage coming out of its casing, and shimmy sideways along the wall like a "Mission Impossible" spy.

Clearly, The Lord is still working on me and my stuff. Slowly, I'm getting there.

How about you? Are you carrying around a suitcase of pavement and treating it like it's gold?

GREED

COLLECTING

Greed makes our priorities a problem.

How many Legos does a kid need to build a cool house? How many crayons are necessary to color a picture: the 8-pack, the 64-pack, or the box of 128 with the built-in sharpener? It seems that we spend an awful lot to make our children--and grandchildren--happy. We associate happiness with giving them more, and more, and more of the things that they want.

If you have children, you have undoubtedly gone into the bedroom, or the playroom, to pick up toys and put them away. How many of the toys never get used, as your child opts for the same one or two whenever playtime comes around? Does their toy box get harder and harder to close because of the accumulation of stuff—whether it's another stuffed animal every Valentine's Day; more plastic eggs at Easter; the fastest and coolest toys at Birthday time; or the number of gifts from Christmas that, by New Years, will be stuck deep in the toy box, never again to see the light of day?

What is true for a child can also be true for the grown up.

I'm not really a collector. I do, however, regularly forget I have something, or I can't find it, so I buy it again. And again. Or, I feel as if I just need one more of "these," in case the first one goes bad. Pretty soon, the adult toy box—my house—is crammed full.

And when I get to that point, I recognize that the thing that at one time *I must have now* has become more of a paperweight or a dust collector than a need.

We consume like crazy. Tools, shoes, soda, hostess gifts, toothpaste, toilet paper--you name it, and we're stocking up on it in order to be prepared, maybe for the next event, maybe for the next catastrophe. The problem is, though, that we want and want and get and get so much that we sometimes forget to live.

Do the things surrounding you have a purpose, or are you

surrounding yourself with them because they make you look or feel a certain way?

A friend has held to a great plan ever since that first child came along. It's called 20 Toys. Not a very creative title, but a very creative philosophy. Each child may have a maximum of 20 toys. Ever. So, if a birthday or Christmas comes around and the child is given a toy, then a choice has to be made: will I keep that gift and give away one of my 20 toys, or will I give that new gift away? It made a huge difference when shopping (well, if you want that stuffed animal, you'll have to make a choice). It has helped that child understand both how to prioritize and how to give. And it has helped to keep the kids' rooms much cleaner than most of our kids' rooms.

What a great philosophy. 20 Toys.

It works for grown-ups, too.

And it's never too late to start.

GREED
BUCKETS

I clearly learned a lot about greed while in Haiti.

One lesson came on our first early-morning of the medical clinic.

There is no electricity in the village we serve. While American teams are camped in the village, a generator is turned on so we have light in the evenings--otherwise, the pitch-black darkness covers the countryside. Even then, at 10 pm, the roar of the generator stops, and we all head to bed, with only the thin streams of the flashlight bulbs to guide us to our tents.

For a moment, let's talk about the bathroom situation.

For many years, all potty breaks were taken in a makeshift porta-potty, built for the visitors. But after dozens of these medical trips, two bathrooms were built. And I mean built. Concrete was poured for a floor, a real flushing toilet was installed in each bathroom, and even a tub was molded from the cement and a shower head was installed. In fact, ours was the first team to use the contemporary bathroom, and the cement had just cured. What a luxury.

Here's the problem: Even with a toilet, a sink, a tub, and a shower head, something was missing.

Water.

An enormous water tank had been installed outside the bathroom. An American architect friend, who was on this team of seven that I was part of, played a large part in making sure it all worked. The biggest challenge was getting the water into the tank, which was hoisted, oh, six feet or so above the ground; this meant that anyone bringing water had to carry the water up a ladder before pouring it into the tank. It was a tremendous feat.

Moreover, the water well was nowhere close. It was outside the main circle of the village, down a steep embankment, and near the trees where we had our Bible classes for the kids. In this heavy rainy season, the only way to get up the hill was to claw nearly hand-and-foot to climb to the top. Someone had to take one of the five-gallon buckets, slide down the hill to the well, fill the bucket, and somehow carry it up the hill, into the camp, past the buildings, past the bathrooms, to the tank area, up the ladder, and hoist the water over the head and pour it into the tank.

That's for five gallons. Seven Americans came on this team (which was about half the size of a regular team).

Saying that water was a luxury is an understatement.

Now, back to that first early-morning of the medical clinic.

At 5 am, I unfolded myself from the pup tent and stepped out into the bright morning Caribbean sunshine. As I walked the path toward the bathroom, I was met by one of the Haitians, carrying one of those five gallon buckets full of water on his head to the water tank. I humbly thanked him as I headed to the bathroom to use that same precious water in what I would consider a spit-bath. The whole time I stood in the tub, and also used the sink to wash my hands, and also flushed the toilet, I watched as that liquid gold went down the drain.

Oh, how I take so much for granted.

But that wasn't the most powerful part of my morning bath. That came as I left the bathroom, now clean and dressed, with a towel wrapped around my wet head. On my way back to the tent, I was met, once again, by the same Haitian, on the same path, again with a full five-gallon bucket, ready to enter the water area where he would again climb the ladder and pour the water into the tank.

I couldn't believe the graciousness of this man, as he had gone, not once, but twice to fill the bucket...all for us. In French, I thanked him and told him that I wasn't sure I would be able to make it through that obstacle course for the water even once, much less twice. I was so grateful for his actions, and I told him so. Humbly, without looking me in the eye, he told me this was not the second time he had gone to get the water for us this morning.

It was his fifth.

As my eyes welled up with tears of gratitude for this man and embarrassment for what these Haitians must be thinking about the Americans that are so used to such luxuries, I had no words to say that would be appropriate. I bowed my head, whispered "thank you" in French, and somehow made it to my tent before the tears spilled out.

As you go about the course of your day, think about what you consider to be necessities: water, electricity, fast food, whatever. When I think to remember that, on this day, in many places in our world, these items are considered luxuries (or things only dreamed about), I am a little less intent on taking them for granted, or hoarding them. I also remember the man who carried the 5 buckets of water...for me.

How can I repay his kindness by carrying that sort of burden for another person today?

How might you?

GREED

AMERICAN GREED

I was quickly hooked on the television show, "American Greed." Each episode described a person, or a group, that works hard to bilk unsuspecting people or organizations out of often millions of dollars. Regularly, these crooks form companies and create elaborate and complicated schemes to lure their prey where the victims are most vulnerable: usually around retirement.

Every once in a while, one of these scoundrels actually sets out to create a fake company and from they start they are off and running to clean out their victims' life savings. Usually, however, these thieves begin as legitimate businessmen that go astray. Typically, one successful sleight of hand results in a payoff, and down the road they go.

I find it curious that many of these scams have a time limit--pay $100,000 into the "investment" now, and in four years, we'll pay out $145,000. But four years later, no money arrives, and the crook is still doing his thing, apparently not recognizing that he's going to get caught. On the show, these guys seem to have no intention of stopping what they're doing, or figuring that anyone's going to actually come knocking on their door.

Why is that?

At first I thought it was pride; these thieves must think they are so good that they're above being found out, even as millions of dollars are being sucked from their victims. But, after watching a number of episodes, I realized that it's not pride. It's almost entirely greed.

Greed gets hold of the heart, and it won't let go. *C'mon, just one more deal. One more day. One more dollar.*

John D. Rockefeller, Sr., lived from the mid-1800s to the mid-1900s. He was an American industrialist and philanthropist. For a time, he was the richest man in the world. He believed his purpose in life was the make as much money as he could, and then use it to improve the world--lofty goal, right? Even so, he is often remembered by the response he gave when he was asked, "How much money is enough?"

He replied, "Just a little bit more."

This was a man who, later in life, handed out dimes to every child he met in the street (during the Depression he began handing out nickels instead). He began his practice of giving with his first paycheck, returning a tenth to his church. As his wealth grew, so did the percentage--and breadth--of his giving. He is responsible for the forming and growth of numerous universities, advances in medicine and technology, and a new model for philanthropy. And yet, as biographer Ron Chernow wrote, "What makes him problematic—and why he continues to inspire ambivalent reactions—is that his good side was every bit as good as his bad side was bad. Seldom has history produced such a contradictory figure."

Before you judge him too quickly, look in the mirror. Plenty of us wish we could make more money so we might give more away. Have you ever thought that? If so, think about this: maybe you already do. Rather than wishing for more (which is at the heart of greed), maybe you could think about giving up something in order to give to others. Maybe it's choosing water instead of soda, then donating the soda money to a ministry you have a heart for. Maybe it's paying off any debt a little faster than planned, which will allow you financial freedom to do more good for the world. Maybe it's going through your bathroom and donating all your extra toiletries to a local half-way house or mission. Maybe it's combing through your closets and donating your extra clothes (this one hits home for me).

Paul wrote these great words of assurance in Philippians 4:19: "And my God will meet all your needs according to the riches of his glory in Christ Jesus."

Most of us have way more than we need.

We don't need to wish for a little bit more.

GREED
THE RAINBOW

One day, I was driving my pre-teen daughter somewhere with her friends. In a rare moment when they were all willing to talk with the old lady in the car, I asked what they wanted to be when they grow up. My daughter said she hadn't narrowed it down quite yet (and was stressing over the fact that she hadn't already determined her life's path). I can't remember what the second girl said; that's because the response from the third girl floored me.

"I want to be a philanthropist."

Did I mention these girls were twelve?

I asked, "Do you know what a philanthropist is?"

"Yes. A philanthropist helps make the world better by donating scads of money for good causes."

"How will be you getting this money that you will then give?"

"Well, of course I will have a great job to earn my millions."

So, it appears that all of the details have not entirely been worked out on her philanthropic hopes and dreams, but the intention is still there. And there's something to be admired about a young person having these kinds of ideals. In fact, I would venture that many of us would like to make buckets of money so we could donate scads of it (although I'm not sure the metric weight of a "scad").

The challenge comes in that we never seem to have enough to get to the scads that we want to donate. We pray and work and search to find the pot of gold at the end of the rainbow, but, if we can find that elusive arch, something happens: GREED. The tricky thing about greed is that we think we can pray and work and search and sometimes even get to the end of the rainbow...and then shift gears and appreciate what we have.

But it's really a gear we don't shift into.

More often, we sort of "absorb" that extra ourselves, then go out in search for another rainbow and another pot.

Instead of seeking the rainbow, what if you were to see the pot of gold you're already standing in? Very few of us will become the Rockefellers of the world, but most of us can still give from the treasure we have right now.

How about a yard sale, where you donate the proceeds? How about giving your time for something? Can you give a dollar to a great cause... and then stretch it to two?

In the same way that we become used to spending more, we can get used to spending less.

That's being a good steward, and it's what the apostle Peter meant when he wrote in 1 Peter 4:9, "Use whatever gift you have received to serve others, as faithful stewards of God's grace in its various forms."

And it's not as difficult to do as you might think.

When I think about it (and I don't have to think too hard), I can pretty easily come up with some easy and not incredibly life-altering ideas to get money.

I could have a glass of water instead of that Super-Family-Fun-Gulp of soda, and set the money aside and donate it. After all, the soda isn't helping me or anyone else, but the dollar I don't spend is a dollar I can give (that's where that quote "a penny saved is a penny earned" comes into play).

That bag of chips that I almost unknowingly down while I'm watching television--I could forego that snack, which is helping me on zero levels, and take that 2 bucks and put it in my donation jar.

Maybe I don't need that thirteenth white blouse that looks like the other twelve that are sitting in my closet, and instead I deposit the money (from the shirt I didn't buy) into my rapidly growing donation jar.

I'll bet I could encourage my kids in a donation challenge, to see what little things we could be doing to change the world.

I think I just found my rainbow.

How about you?

GREED

WHAT'S IMPORTANT

What's most important to you?

I would like to say that my priorities are in order.

But when I think back on just the early portion of each day, I get a little different picture of what's important.

30 minutes of Bible reading and writing start the day. Good priority.

This, of course, is followed by 45 minutes of getting ready. Then another half hour of trying on 8 outfits in order to make just the right clothing choice; I'd like to say that I'm looking for something that will reflect my attitude for that day, but the fact is that my attitude is always the same: I want to put on something that makes me look skinny, athletic, beautiful, confident, trendy, classy, exotic, and mysterious. At the last minute, I'm pushing the kids out the door as and throwing them each a Pop-Tart (breakfast of champions), yelling that they're going to be late for school. And don't flunk the math test. And come home right after school. And don't forget your backpack. Oh, and I love you. I am now late, so I forget to take out the trash or feed the dog. Somewhere in all of this, my husband has left for work...did I kiss him good-bye? Did I give him the cup of coffee I poured for him before I became frantic? I can't remember.

When I get home from work, I see the remnants of my morning: the seven outfits I didn't wear are in various stages of disarray in the bedroom, crumpled and needing to be ironed...again. The cup of coffee I lovingly made for my husband still sits, full, on the counter--I guess that answers that question. The dog has been practicing his new trick of tipping over the kitchen trash can, so last night's dinner scraps are strewn about the kitchen...and the dining room...and the living room (at least they're not in the bathroom, but that's only because the dog won't go in there because terrible things like baths take place in that torture chamber).

What's more, by tomorrow morning, I will have forgotten what I wore today, and the process will start all over.

What really matters? What's important?

I can look back on any span of time and remember that I have wasted an awful lot of time worrying about clothing, food, and money. But I don't remember that stressing about any of those things actually helped. There actually may be something to Jesus saying those key words in Matthew 6:

> *25 "Therefore I tell you, do not worry about your life, what you will eat or drink; or about your body, what you will wear. Is not life more than food, and the body more than clothes? 26 Look at the birds of the air; they do not sow or reap or store away in barns, and yet your heavenly Father feeds them. Are you not much more valuable than they? 27 Can any one of you by worrying add a single hour to your life[e]?*

> *28 "And why do you worry about clothes? See how the flowers of the field grow. They do not labor or spin. 29 Yet I tell you that not even Solomon in all his splendor was dressed like one of these. 30 If that is how God clothes the grass of the field, which is here today and tomorrow is thrown into the fire, will he not much more clothe you— you of little faith? 31 So do not worry, saying, 'What shall we eat?' or 'What shall we drink?' or 'What shall we wear?' 32 For the pagans run after all these things, and your heavenly Father knows that you need them. 33 But seek first his kingdom and his righteousness, and all these things will be given to you as well. 34 Therefore do not worry about tomorrow, for tomorrow will worry about itself. Each day has enough trouble of its own.*

Clothes, food, and money are hot buttons of worry for me. And not one is important to the kingdom of God.

For today, I'll spend less time staring in the closet and more time walking with The Lord, hanging out with my family, and not being frantic about what proportion of cotton/poly blend I'll be wearing.

That's my plan, anyway. Lord, I'll need your help to make it happen.

How could you use His help today?

GREED
STILL LEARNING THE LESSON

I'm a repeat offender when it comes to worrying about what I'm going to wear. Unfortunately, my mishaps are good examples of what not to do, so, more than a little ashamedly, I will share this story with you:

A number of years ago, I bought a dress. I've purchased a number of dresses in my lifetime, but this one was special. I ordered it online, but then I couldn't fit into it, so I put it in my closet, hoping that one day I might be able to pour myself into it. Then, a couple of years later, I pulled it out of the closet and tried it on, surprised that it looked like it might actually fit.

A little self-conscious, I decided to ask the fashion guru of our household if she thought it was appropriate for me to wear. So I found Mary Jo (who was 4 at the time), who was a little frustrated that I was interrupting her Sesame Street experience, and I asked her if she liked my outfit. First, she rolled her eyes and gave me that sigh—if you are a parent, you can easily picture this. Then, realizing that she wasn't going to get rid of me until she did her duty, she got up and faced me. Starting at my head, she scrutinized every inch of me as her eyes wandered down to my shoes. Then, she started back up to my face. Then she began looking down again, and finally she looked up into my eyes. After a pregnant pause when she was perfectly still, she ended with this: "Ehh… It's fine." Then she went back to Sesame Street.

Is it really that important for me to have fashion confirmation from my four-year-old before I'll walk out the door? Apparently, at least on that day, it was.

You should have heard what she said on another day when she didn't like an outfit— "Oh, Mommy, you should change right now. And I'll wait for you."

And she did. And I did. Because I was so desperate to look good.

You may be thinking that this sounds like insecurity rather than greed. In some ways, you'd be right. I'm unsure about myself, so I want to present my outsides in a way that will reflect how I want to feel on the inside.

But greed is the same in that regard. I want more because I'm insecure. I don't trust God enough to handle it, and, in fact, every time I try to make a suggestion about how this or that could be done better, He seems to have changed the channel and is listening to another station.

I want more, says the Greedy One. *I don't trust that God's going to take care of the situation, and I'll be happy with just a little bit more.*

Problem is, there's always a little more to try to get. And then life becomes an endless pursuit of that little bit more—even if it seems like it's just about an outfit.

I don't have it all down. But The Lord is working on me, and I want to live my life to its fullest, in honor of Him.

I know it all sounds silly--worrying about clothing. I do have other things to be anxious about, like whether my kids will grow up to be mature and responsible and Jesus-followers (and not stress over the silly things their mom does). I worry about making ends meet and often stress over the electricity bill.

But if I can give The Lord my anxiety about one thing, why can't I give Him all of it? He says He'll take it and lighten my load.

Why, then, would I choose to hold on to such obnoxious worry that carries no value, adds no joy, and gives me no purpose?

Why would you?

GREED

WAITING TO BE WORTHWHILE

A man was given an unexpected $100 bonus at work. He wanted to give a portion to The Lord, so he said to himself, "I'm going to buy $100 worth of lottery tickets. With whatever my winnings are, half will go to The Lord. That way, I'll be doing something really worthwhile."

Clearly, you get the sideways thinking here. Instead of "letting it ride," the man could have given half of his bonus to The Lord.

Let's just say that he took that money, bought some tickets, and won. Then what? Would he stop, or would he try again for even more?

The amount isn't what matters to The Lord; the heart is.

Do you look at what you have, and make plans to give to The Lord "once I have more"? Instead, how about considering: What does The Lord desire of me...with where I am right this very moment, and with what I currently have?

Greed can be so subtle.

I remember my college years, when I scraped up enough quarters to do the laundry so I'd have a clean shirt...rather than today, when I'm dipping into my slush fund for that cute top that I don't need but try to convince myself I do. In those early adult years, I longed for a bus pass so I wouldn't have to walk to the grocery store a couple of miles away. Now I get upset when I see that someone scratched the paint on my very nice car.

Greed can be so subtle.

As time passes, the appetite for things increases. We may have all the intentions of trying to do something good with our lives—if only I could get rich, then I'll give it to God—but we forget that we ARE rich. And we don't need to wait until we have more.

I was rich when I could scrape up enough money for the laundry. I'm rich now, too.

A famous morning show host was being interviewed. The host quietly sat, eyes down, as the interviewer read aloud the host's recently published salary, which was in the millions. The host was gentle but quick to state that it's expensive to live in New York and to live the life of a celebrity--drivers and events and homes and outfits and flights and the like.

Yup. Must be tough. I thought, Oh, what I could do with that extra money...I could help others, build schools, fight hunger, get hurting people off the street...it's too bad she wastes so much of that money on things that are fleeting.

But then the Lord tapped me on the figurative shoulder and reminded me: I'll bet others would feel the same way about me, especially when they saw that I get lazy some days and stop to pick up a pizza for dinner, and often we eat on what we like to call Fine China (paper plates) because I don't feel like doing dishes, and I excessively stock up on Band-Aids (I like to justify that there's a Band-Aid for every kind of cut, so why not use the proper one?), and I have more than one pair of shoes (and more than one dozen pair of shoes), and I buy in bulk when there's a sale (and sometimes when there isn't), and I purchase lots of things I don't need, and I live in a nice house for four people when I know others that cram a dozen people into a hut that's smaller than the living room I hardly use, and...and...and on, and on, and on.

Oh, the conviction I feel. I am getting bonuses, surprises, treasures in my life regularly, and I far too often wait to "turn that into some real money so I can share it with The Lord."

For today, I want to intentionally find a way to give something extra to The Lord, not when I get more, but right now.

Are you with me?

GREED

'TIS THE SEASON

It was December in a house with a 9-year-old and a 6-year-old. That meant it was the season for shopping, for school parties, and for the giant Christmas lists of must-haves that at least my kids write. That particular year our 2 children began making out their Christmas lists on Thanksgiving Day. It was the first time that either of them read through the entire newspaper, in search of every possible toy in every possible ad. My daughter emphatically explained that she had gone through the whole paper and "circled up" every item that she wanted. I could then transpose each item on her Christmas list, "So get moving, Mom."

That went over well.

After a long conversation where I helped her understand that I am, in fact, not her servant, I thought I would go through the newspaper and see what, in fact, she had "circled up."

She had "circled up" everything. Every item. You *know* how many ads there are in the newspaper on Thanksgiving Day, right? When I went looking for the kids to talk about the importance of giving over receiving, I found them both, about 6 inches from the television, Christmas lists in hand, just waiting for each commercial so Ben could write every item down—girl items on Mary's list, boy items on Ben's list.

The television went off for a while so we could talk about Christmas.

We have a Christmas rule in our house: three gifts. Each child gets three main gifts. After all, Jesus got three gifts: gold, frankincense, and myrrh; since we're celebrating His birthday, then we can celebrate the same way, with three gifts. In moments of frustration during that time of year, you might hear the phrase "Do you think you deserve more than Jesus?" coming from somewhere in the house. Of course, the three-gift rule doesn't take into consideration stocking stuffers and grandparents, but it's still a good rule, or at least a guide, to try to follow. So, I told the kids, "You might want to be careful about what you put on your list. If we're only going to get you three gifts, then you'll want to be sure that we get what you want."

Mary Jo unfolded herself from her criss-cross-applesauce position, got up, walked over and faced me, and put her hand on my shoulder. In her most compassionate voice, she said, "It's okay, Mom. You can choose whatever three gifts you want. Santa will get the rest of the things on my list for me."

That moment, something became clear: we had a long way to go.

Greed can sneak up on the best and most innocent of us. It is pervasive in our world...and on our televisions. But take heart: it does NOT have to become the standard in our homes, where Jesus is wanting to set the standard.

Snagging the shiniest gifts that won't be remembered come New Year's Day is not the point of Christmas. Loving The Lord, and showing that love by giving to others--that's the point. Christmas should be the biggest birthday party of the year, because it's the celebration of the greatest gift-giver of all: Jesus.

GREED

PHENOMENAL

I can admit it, before God and you as my witness. I honestly thought that I was about to receive my ten minutes of fame, and in just the way I was wanting it.

Here was the situation.

I got a phone call from a reporter from our local newspaper. The reporter was working on a story about a woman I knew very well, a dear saint in our church whose autobiography was recently completed. I learned from the reporter that I was one of the first people he'd contacted.

That piqued both my interest and enthusiasm.

The reporter spent, what—twenty, thirty—minutes on the phone with me, typing like the wind as I talked to be sure he actually wrote every single word I said so that I might not be misquoted. I told stories of first meeting her when I was eleven years old, I ran through different memories I had of this spit of a woman that had command of every activity she was responsible for, I described her ability to serve others of all ages as she served the Lord, I described her deep interest in children and her call to help raise up pastors' children in the way they should go.

And the reporter was clearly tracking with me. I was paying attention to his typing as I was talking, and he was right with me. He then asked if he could attend something where she might be doing her "thing." I told him to come to the Senior Luncheon the next week.

So he did. He took pictures of her as she assisted with the food, he talked to other people, he asked me more questions, he even stayed until the end of the luncheon.

And, I admit it. I thought I was about to receive my accolades as the main source of information for this article.

And then the article came out. My mom called me and told me to look in the paper that Friday. Sure, I wanted to read all about this saint, certainly, but I really wanted to see how much of the great material I gave was used. I opened it up, scanned the article, and came to <u>my</u> quote.

The reporter stated my name and said I can sum her up as—and here's my quote—"phenomenal."

Phenomenal. One word. I read to the bottom of the column, then the next column, then the next, then I turned the page…nothing.

One word. Phenomenal.

And my ten minutes of fame became ten letters of fame, and it was over. Ten letters? Where are all my musings? Where's that great illustration that leads you to laugh…and cry? Where's my…my…

Oh, my.

How humbling. And revealing as, once again, I'd made something all about me, when it should have been all about her.

Will I ever learn?

GREED

ICE BAG

When you're expecting one thing but receive another, you may find it easy to overlook the first thing as a gift.

But that's the challenge with this and all the other deadly sins. They're all about ME, which means at their foundation they are flawed.

I had hurt my back, and I was having a hard time getting out of bed the next day. I heard a noise in the next room and thought it was my husband, so I yelled out, "Could you bring me a baggy of ice?"

A few minutes later, my 4-year-old came into the room with her hands behind her back. I said, "Good morning," and she said, "Hi, Mommy. I heard you needed this a LOT…" and from behind her back, she pulled out a giant, gallon-size baggy, with two ice cubes inside.

Best ice pack ever.

Who cares that this giant baggy of mostly air ever would melt in a matter of minutes?

What an unexpected gift of love…and a salve to my soul.

The Lord is waiting to give you a gift today…perhaps in a way, or in a package, that you are not expecting at all. Don't forget to keep your eyes—and your heart—open to seeing His gift to you.

GREED

FUTURE PLANS

Is this greed, or is this pride? You decide.

When our dog was a puppy, she liked to find any clothing within reach (amazing what a dog can reach, right?), and drag it into the living room so she could be surrounded by the familiar smell of family. It was an adorable habit…right up until she would bring clothes into the living room while we had company. Some clothing simply shouldn't be seen by company.

We humans are not much different. We like to surround ourselves with our stuff in order to be comforted and to feel at peace. We often forget that it's just stuff.

The stuff of life is similar. We are pretty willing to talk about our plans; to talk about our future; to talk about our families, jobs, travel, accomplishments, retirement.

But, while we don't know exactly the avenue it will take, and whether we will be successful or not, or whether we will get sick or not, or whether we will travel the world or stay in our own little neck of it, there is one thing we can be sure of: it will end. We don't know how, but, if we are like every other person on the planet since the dawn of time [except for those two fellows in the Old Testament, one who was no more (Enoch) and one who rode a chariot to heaven (Elijah)], then we can plan on this life ending for us.

So, why aren't we more open about it and live our best lives, knowing that this life will, in fact, have an end? Instead, we continue to surround ourselves with our stuff, thinking that those things grant us peace.

Every day I get to be part of conversations—the sorts of conversations that really matter, because they are shared by folks that know their time on earth is limited, so they want to make the most out of every moment and live in the best way possible.

Just because we choose not to talk about something doesn't mean it won't happen. And just because I surround myself with my stuff doesn't mean I'm going to be able to keep it forever.

Let go of one thing you're holding onto today. Find peace in thinking about how you're going to live your life in the best way you can on this day, and recognize that your legacy can be a tremendous gift for those you love. Help prepare those close to you for the future, because the best is yet to come…well after this life is over.

CHAPTER SEVEN: SLOTH— IT'S NOT MY JOB

SLOTH
MY HANDS DON'T SEEM TO BE IDLE

Revelation 3:14-22, The Church in Laodicea
To the Church in Laodicea

¹⁴"To the angel of the church in Laodicea write:

These are the words of the Amen, the faithful and true witness, the ruler of God's creation. ¹⁵I know your deeds, that you are neither cold nor hot. I wish you were either one or the other! ¹⁶So, because you are lukewarm—neither hot nor cold—I am about to spit you out of my mouth. ¹⁷You say, 'I am rich; I have acquired wealth and do not need a thing.' But you do not realize that you are wretched, pitiful, poor, blind and naked. ¹⁸I counsel you to buy from me gold refined in the fire, so you can become rich; and white clothes to wear, so you can cover your shameful nakedness; and salve to put on your eyes, so you can see. ¹⁹Those whom I love I rebuke and discipline. So be earnest, and repent. ²⁰Here I am! I stand at the door and knock. If anyone hears my voice and opens the door, I will come in and eat with him, and he with me. ²¹To him who overcomes, I will give the right to sit with me on my throne, just as I overcame and sat down with my Father on his throne. ²²He who has an ear, let him hear what the Spirit says to the churches."

Sloth. The word even <u>sounds</u> sluggish.

A sloth is a typically tree-dwelling critter found in Central and South America. It is a distant relative of the armadillo and the anteater. Sloths live in tropical forests, where they sleep, eat, and travel through the trees suspended upside-down, clinging to branches with the powerful curved claws of their forelimbs and hindlimbs. Algae that grow on the hair give the coat a greenish tint to blend with its surroundings. Sloths move sluggishly but can strike swiftly and powerfully if attacked.

That's what a sloth—the animal—is. Take away the climbing upside-down through the trees and add a couch and a bag of potato chips, and you know what we're talking about as one of the deadly sins.

The deadly sin of sloth is the avoidance of physical or spiritual or emotional work. It's extreme laziness. Spiritual apathy. An attitude of *I don't feel like it right now*, or of *I gave at the office*, or *I've already done enough.*

Here's our challenge: The Lord has a plan for us...and it includes our participation. In Matthew 28, after the resurrection, Jesus doesn't tell the disciples, "Here I am, alive! Now, go ahead and hang out at the local watering well and talk about the glory days of what you experienced. No need to take any action in your lives."

No way! Jesus tells them, "I'm more powerful than you ever guessed. So don't be lazy; get on your feet...and GO! I gave you life, so go live it to its fullest, making every moment count. Go tell people about me. Be my representatives by living, really living; in these last few years together, I've taught you how. So don't be Sabbath Christians and week-long atheists. Spread the word by the way you live, showing love, building relationships, and preaching the good news. And, when it's really necessary, use words" (that's my paraphrase of Matthew 28).

The worst thing in the world isn't in not knowing The Lord. The worst thing is knowing The Lord but not doing anything about it. If your friends can't tell that you're a Christian, something's wrong. And that something isn't them.

One way the sin of sloth eeks into our lives is when we're so busy doing other things that we don't have time--or don't want to make the time--for God-inspired, God-thanking, God-loving things. We were created to love The Lord and love our neighbors; when we stray from those things, or practice them in the wrong priority (loving God inspires us to love our neighbor, which turns us back to loving God), then our little spiritually lazy friend may be lurking nearby.

A challenge with being a sloth (other than it's not an attractive trait) is that, when you exhibit sloth-like behavior, you begin wasting away, like spiritual atrophy, which affects you and those around you. Spiritual atrophy is similar to muscle atrophy. If you don't use your muscles, then they get weak, and you're not able to do all you were made to do-- whether it's running a marathon or cleaning out the attic. If you let your muscles take a vacation, then you won't be prepared for high-energy tasks...or high-energy fun. The same can be said about spiritual atrophy.

Another issue with being spiritually lazy is that you open the door for sin. "Idle hands are the devil's tools"--this quote probably originated from Chaucer, who quotes St. Jerome in The Canterbury Tales. When we are about the Lord's work, we won't remain idle. When we get lazy, we open the door for the devil to come in and use us for his glory instead of God's glory. And that's not good.

Perhaps you think, once again, that this sin, the sin of sloth, doesn't pertain to you. This one I knew I had in the bag, <u>finally</u>. This one is so very not me, which is nice at the end of this long series, where I have been continually confronted by deadly sins I never knew I actually harbored. But this time, I was certain my name was nowhere near this sin--because I am so busy all the time, and am actually criticized for not relaxing. I figured you may be on your own on this one.

Again.

And again...I was wrong.

Eugene Peterson wrote a great book for pastors called "Working the Angles." He focuses on three pastoral acts that make up the angles of the triangle of ministry, which many--one might contend that most-- pastors have abandoned: prayer, Scripture, and spiritual direction. They are disciplines that are done, not in public, like the Sunday morning leading of worship, but in quiet, relationship-building acts between God, pastor, and people.

Peterson contends that, instead, pastors have, for the most part, become "a company of shopkeepers, and the shops they keep are churches. They are preoccupied with shopkeeper's concerns--how to keep customers happy, how to lure customers away from competitors down the street, how to package the goods so that the customers will lay out more money."

Pastors are busy. If you are a churchgoer, or a pastor, take note:

being busy is not the goal. The Lord has a plan for us to live life to its fullest, not to simply spin our wheels. If a pastor is so focused on being the shopkeeper Peterson describes, he (or she) very well may not be focused on the key angles of ministry and may miss the point altogether. These disciplines are typically found in purposeful quiet, in listening, in humble teach-back, in grace-filled learning. And remember: being quiet is not laziness; in fact, often the one running around with his head cut off may be the most slothful, because he is wasting his purpose on meaningless tasks.

We can deceive ourselves into thinking that we are anything but lazy for the Lord. In actuality, however, we are often so far off the mark that God wouldn't be proud of the work we do for Him, because we're not taking care of what He's already given us: a home, a family, pets, a job, a calling--you name it. And He knows it. Plus, when we're sloth-like, we're an example of the sort of Christian that non-Christians are so used to seeing: the hypocritical and lazy believer. Why would anyone want to participate in that sort of faith?

Let's jump in together and learn about the sin of sloth...or slothfulness...or slothdom...or whatever you want to call it.

I have a feeling I may resemble a claw-grabbing tree-dweller more than I care to admit.

SLOTH

TRACK

My daughter was preparing to turn out for track--her first foray into competitive sports. The only problem is that, unlike the adults in our family, she's not competitive. "All my friends are turning out for track, Mom. Besides, as long as I stick with it, I'm in. It's 'no-cut' track."

Her attitude about track was admirable, and she was ready...right up until the night before track started. Needing some back-up, I took her to my parents' house; I figured Poppa and Grandma, who have seen their four children through every sport in the book, would have good insight.

And boy, was I right. Mary explained that she didn't need to be the best runner on the team. She just didn't want to embarrass herself. My dad sat across from Mary, and he said this: "Mary Jo, picture you with a friend, out in the woods. All of a sudden, a mean and hungry bear comes on the scene, and he has you and your friend in his sites as the best next snack. The trick is knowing this: You don't have to run faster than the bear.

"You only have to run faster than your friend."

I'm not really sure that this is an example of appropriate Christian behavior, but it got Mary more comfortable, and she made it through the first track meet just fine.

Then kids started to drop off the team.

Mary had been placed on the fourth relay squad on her team (which made sense, since she was neither experienced nor competitive). But a few days before the next meet, one of the girls on the first relay squad was unable to run in the meet. Since one of Mary's friends was on that first squad, the friend asked the coach if Mary could be the sub for that one meet.

Curiously, the coach said, "Sure."

I think I was more nervous the day of the meet than Mary was. Unfortunately, the meet was some distance away, and I was unable to drive to the event. So I had to wait until she got home before she could give the play-by-play.

She walked into the house, sat down in the living room where the rest of us were waiting, and she stated emphatically, "Well, we were disqualified."

Oh, no.

"Don't worry, Mom, it wasn't because of me. I ran second, and it went fine. I passed the baton to the girl that ran third, and she did fine. But when the baton was passed from the third to the fourth runner, they dropped the baton, so we got DQ'd."

I was so relieved.

"Oh, and one more thing," Mary calmly stated. "It was so weird being on the first relay squad. I had to run so much faster than when I'm on the fourth squad. Well, time for a snack. Later."

And off she went.

Of all the things that have surprised me about this season's track experience, it was that last statement that I've come back to time and time again. "I had to run so much faster than when I'm on the fourth squad."

What a great example of sticking with the crowd. Mary wasn't running on a particular squad <u>because</u> of her speed; she made her speed comparable to the squad she was on. Had she never been placed as a sub on the first squad, nobody would have ever known that she <u>could</u> run faster.

The sin of sloth enters when you stick with status quo. When you do what's expected and nothing more.

It never dawned on Mary to try to run her fastest when she was on the fourth relay squad. That may be the case for you, too; whether it's at work, at home, in your marriage, in your friendships, in your finances, in your gardening, in all things, perhaps you're so used to just hanging with the crowd that you have forgotten to step it up, to do your best, to "run in such a way as to get the prize" (1 Corinthians 9:24).

I'm not sure if Mary will try out for track in the future, but I am sure that her experience was a lesson for her...and me.

SLOTH
IT'S NOT MY JOB!

I served a church in the Midwest that boasted 1,000 members, but we had zero members between the ages of 19 and 35. The parents who had adult children of those ages couldn't figure out why they weren't able to get their kids to stay in the church once those kids reached adulthood. After all, when their children were younger, the parents took them to church every week. Yup, they drove them to the church every Sunday, dropped them off, and let the kids go into the basement and play cards during the worship service. Some of those kids were there *all morning*...so the parents just couldn't understand why their kids never learned to cling to the Bible or the church.

See the problem?

Maybe it's because the parents assumed the kids would learn it through osmosis, not through worship and Sunday school and a family life where they were learning how to be faithful followers of Christ.

Sloth is presuming that training my kids to be followers of The Lord is someone else's responsibility. As a parent, I could be adamant and question the church leadership, "Why isn't somebody teaching my children in Sunday school?" At the same time, I need to be asking, "Am I teaching them about The Lord every day?" After all, it is my responsibility to raise my kids up in the way I should go, so says the Proverb, "and when they are old, they will not depart from it" (Proverbs 22:6). I'd better be doing something other than pointing the finger of responsibility at others, because that finger quickly morphs into the powerful, curved claw of the two-toed sloth.

Every time we have a baptism at church, I have an opportunity to see faith in action. When an infant is being baptized, I get to hear the parents declare that they love Jesus Christ and will raise this child up under the shade of the loving arm of the Lord. I watch and wonder if the baby will laugh or cry as the water is doused on him. We all *oooh* and *aaah* at the cute little outfit and the even cuter little dimples.

But in a baptism, we as a family of believers are doing something more than all of that. As we sit in the pew and watch all that's going on, we are more than spectators. We are participants. In fact, every time you witness a baptism, you are challenged to remember your own baptism and what Jesus has done for you so that you can be washed clean of your sin. And every time a baby is baptized, at least in the church I go to, we participants are asked this question:

Do you, the people of the church, promise to tell this child the good news of the gospel, to help him know all that Christ commands, and, by your fellowship, to strengthen his family ties with the household of God?

Together, we answer, "*We do.*" Just remember this: when you don't follow through on this promise, then you are practicing the deadly sin of sloth.

Look around you today. Who have you had an opportunity to make an impression upon? Have you crossed paths with someone and stepped aside, or have you chosen to take the time—and the energy—to build a relationship with them? Every conversation that you have, every phone call that you make, every note that you write, every person that you confront is an opportunity to rid yourself of sloth and be filled with—and share—the love of the Lord Himself.

What are you waiting for?

SLOTH

LUKEWARM LIVING

Why do you think that we often treat our work in the church the same way we treat our work in the world? When we do say yes to serving in the church, why does it seem to come out of guilt instead out of gratitude?

Who doesn't see those pictures of Cleopatra, whose servants wave palm fronds gently over her draped body, and whose maids feed her peeled grapes one by one, and think: Man, the only peeled grapes I ever get are the ones little Johnny splattered the nursery wall with last week during snack time?

I'm in college. I have my whole life ahead of me. Right now, I've got studies, I've got classes, I've got friends to hang with…this is my time. Once I get "established," then I'll help in the church.

I'm tired. I've had a whole week of work. I've had to come home to a dirty house, spend my evenings cleaning dirty kids, go to work in a dirty car, and be inundated with dirty business. Who has time for more work?

I'll help in the church when I retire.

I have spent my life in the church. Now that I'm retired, I finally have time for myself. I'm going to travel, I'm going to sit, and I'm going to finally do some things for _me_.

Let the younger ones help in the church. I've done my time.

Want to see a church on fire? Then look at who is really running it: the members who are being fueled by Christ to serve in whatever way He sees fit, not whatever way _I_ see fit.

Lukewarm Christians make for a lukewarm church.

If the Westminster Larger Catechism is right, and *Man's chief and highest end is to glorify God, and fully to enjoy him forever*, then I'm not in this life to store up my treasures for retirement, or work so I can be lazy down the road, or even be lazy and just hope that something good will fall from the sky for me. I'm in this life for God—to be a mirror for God to the world, to be the hands and feet of Jesus, and to finally learn that the only true joy that comes out of life is the joy of enjoying Him fully, in whatever manner He decides.

At least nonbelievers take a stand. At least you know that they aren't coming to church, and you can't make them. Even the nonbeliever has a conviction: he won't darken the door of the church.

But what's worse than the nonbeliever is the Lukewarm Christian.

Laodicea was a city of wealth, a city that was an important center of trade and communication. But it was also a city that's difficult to describe, because not one thing stands out.

The people of Laodicea had learned to compromise; they did not zealously stand for anything. When we don't zealously stand for anything, then we become lukewarm like them. That makes us slothful.

Does that make you angry—that your energy might be questioned? Then ask yourself these questions:

- What am I doing for the Lord (not for myself, but for the Lord) today?
- What am I doing in the name of the Lord that I would still be doing if nobody else in the world saw me doing it?
- Who am I truly making an impression on for Jesus?
- In my teaching, or my preaching, or my advising, or my helping, am I really serving the cause of Christ or my own causes?

A friend took a tour through the Seven Churches of Revelation. They traveled through Turkey, walking a lot. When they got to Laodicea, they read the passage from Revelation 3 about how the people's deeds were known, and they were neither cold nor hot. My friend showed me a picture of the city, which is on a hill. About 5 miles south of the front of the city are a slew of hot springs, and steam rises from below. Above the city are salt formations that look like snow-capped mountains. Anyone looking at the city and hearing these words from Revelation would immediately make the connection, because the town looked both cold (from the look of snow above) and hot (from the hot springs below), and itself is actually neither. Also, since a vast expanse of aqueducts was created to bring the water in from the hot springs, by the time the water reached the city, it was never more than lukewarm. Neither hot...nor cold.

There is nothing worse than being lukewarm. Lukewarm coffee isn't even good enough to spit out. A lukewarm bath isn't refreshing. A lukewarm handshake leaves much to be desired. And a lukewarm Christian can do more to harm the cause of Christ than to expand it.

Find a way to be zealous for the Lord today. You just may find that your life may look a lot different by the end of the day.

SLOTH

LAZY WITH PERSONALITY

My son has this ability to change his stature at the blink of an eye (or the command of a mom). He can go from energetic, excited, and happy to losing every motor skill and collapsing onto the couch in three monosyllabic words:

Clean your room.

Once I'm able to revive him and get him back on his feet and heading toward his room, he emits a half-growl/half-sigh and begins the 10-minute (and 10-yard) walk of doom toward his bedroom. You would think he was walking the Long Green Mile.

As any parent knows, this is not the end of the story, for I must check in on him every few minutes to remind him that he is to be cleaning his room—not sleeping, not listening to music, not playing on his i-whatever.

The reply is consistent: "But, Mom, it *is* clean."

At this point in the game, I don't usually know what he's even referring to being clean—the ceiling? Bed: unmade. Desk: can't find it. Carpet: it was blue the last time I saw it, but that's been awhile. He has so much stuff stuffed under his bed that the mattresses are now high-centered over the frame.

I'm so proud.

What's more, it looks as if the dog has been trained to respond similarly to his commands. I tell him that he needs to go outside, and it takes 10 minutes for him to slump over (with that similar combination growl/heavy sigh) and walk the plank out to the yard. You'd think I was torturing him.

See, sloth is an extra-special sort of lazy. It's lazy with personality.

We all get tired. We should all rest. We should be willing to work hard, play hard, and rest, well, well.

Just because you're resting doesn't mean you're a sloth.

Sloth comes about when you commit to something, and you decide not to follow through. It's when you say you'll do something, but then you don't practice what you preach. It's when you make a promise and don't keep it.

Uh-oh. This may not be so far off from my own world.

I'm so busy. I've got tons going on. So, when I commit to being somewhere for a friend but I am unable to make that date, I figure that they'll understand. After all, I'm so busy.

But who ever said that busy is good?

For some reason, people seem to use the phrase, "Oh, you're so busy," to be a compliment. It's not, you know. It's not healthy, it's not how we were created, and it doesn't mean that you have more purpose.

It just means that you haven't organized your time well, and it may mean that you suffer from a lack of peace.

In the 1990 film "Awakenings," Robin Williams is a doctor who uses a new drug, L-Dopa, on patients in a catatonic state, who are then temporarily brought out of the catatonia. There's a scene in the movie where the doctor explains his patients' disease, which looks to be an extreme case of Parkinson's (which is what L-Dopa was actually created to treat). He asks an expert, "Do you think a simple Parkinsonian tremor, taken to its further extreme, would appear as no tremor at all?" See, he's working with these patients that have, for all practical purposes, turned into statues. One of the symptoms of Parkinson's is uncontrolled tremors (which his patients don't have—in fact, just the opposite. They're statues). His theory was that his patients may be shaking so badly, and so fast, that it then appeared that they were not shaking at all.

That thought is what I picture when I think of being overly busy.

If I'm so busy that I'm anxious (Proverbs 12:25 is a good reminder here: "An anxious heart weighs a man down, but a kind word cheers him up"), or I get worried ("Who of you by worrying can add a single hour to his life,"—that one comes from Jesus), and I don't feel peace ("and the peace of Christ will guard your hearts and minds forever"— the Apostle Paul penned this one), then perhaps the busy that I'm busy with isn't the best sort of busy.

Busy work does not equal great work. Working on things that

matter--that's great work. As you look back on your day, take stock of what was really important, what was necessary, and what was busy-work...and what was just plain wasted time.

I regularly get the opportunity to sit with dying patients. So many look back at the time they wasted doing meaningless tasks or sitting in front of the television for days at a time or holding grudges that should have been let go of years before.

The sin of sloth robs us of meaningful life.

Consider making a plan for your day. What is on your agenda to deal with that matters? What can you let go of? What might you discard as meaningless? What can you add that enriches life and builds a relationship?

It's never too late to restart your day.

As long as I have breath, I will praise The Lord.

What greater purpose can there be?

SLOTH
I CAN'T

I'd been dreading it for a decade and a half, but there was no escaping it. The day had finally arrived.

Time to teach my daughter to drive.

Her older brother, Ben, had been a cake-walk to teach. But for some reason, I knew this would be different.

Now, don't get me wrong. She's always been a quick learner. And we have this relationship the likes of which I could have only dreamed of: we actually get along. But I think she may be too smart for her own good.

I think she gets it from her grandmother.

We lived fifteen miles out of town, on a giant hill, over a creek and through the mud to get home. We had a seventeen-year-old Jeep, a manual transmission, that would be the only car Mary would be able to use once she got her license (which is more than many kids get), so there was no better time than now for her to learn the finer points of country driving with a stick shift.

She drove okay at first, albeit timidly, which I suppose is what every parent prefers. But then the snow came, and the ice, and the lack of plowing on those country roads. She was horrified, nearly paralyzed, behind the wheel, afraid she would slide off the road and into the ditch...or down an embankment...or off the face of the earth...or some other sensible thought.

The entrance to our neighborhood started with a quarter-mile incline that had to be taken in four-wheel-drive, often even in summer. The road was sandwiched between the side of a hill and a steep drop-off. One attempt up that hill, and she slipped ever-so-slightly off her chosen path, and Mary swore she would never get behind the wheel again. "You can drive me until I get married," was her rational sentiment.

That seemed a touch dramatic.

We braved the roads that winter. I admit, it was a bit rough, even for the grown-ups. I took her to school each morning, and she somehow found rides home by the end of the day. And each time she passed the tan Jeep, she mumbled a little curse. She declared she would be content to never drive in that "tin can of horror" again.

And each day, I tried to get her to drive it. "Just test it out, you might find you're better at driving it than you think."

No chance.

I started picking her up in the Jeep—foregoing my nicer car with modern amenities—on the chance that she might be willing to get behind the wheel.

She wasn't.

As the weather got warmer, and the snow turned to rain, I made her drive in the Jeep with me on flat roads, even while she let crocodile tears slowly drip from her eyes. As the Central Washington weather got warmer, then turned hot, we took the hard-top off the Jeep for the summer. I wouldn't let her drive my car, though she begged and begged.

And then one Saturday I had to work and some friends invited her to do something, and all she had at home was the Jeep and its key. She texted permission to go out, and of course I said yes. I figured she got a ride with a friend (her friends are saints). I got home from work to find that both she and the Jeep were gone. A little while later, she came pulling into the driveway, bounding up the steps, and flying into the living room, a smile from ear to ear. She plopped into a chair near me, looked me straight in the eyes, and raised one eyebrow slightly, showing her "I know something you don't know" face.

"Okay," I started, "What gives? Clearly, there's a story here."

"Yup," she replied. Then, as if it was a common occurrence, she continued, "Don't know if you noticed, I took the Jeep."

"I did notice. Care to share what happened?"

"Sure. It used to be scary to drive. But the weather changed, then you took the top off, and then I realized, I look GOOD driving this!"

She immediately jumped up and headed to the kitchen for a snack.

"I look good in this."

That's what it took to get her to drive? Not safety lessons, not the fear of failure, not surrounding the car in bubble wrap, but "I look good in this"?

I haven't seen my Jeep since.

Here's the thing. This little story could have gone into nearly any of the Deadly categories. Pride: that one's pretty obvious. Envy: I actually would like to look as good as she does in that Jeep. Lust: I want that car! I could go on. But this story is in the category of Sloth because it's an example of letting fear take over and keep Mary from taking action. It wasn't until she realized that there was an extra benefit to having some independence ("I look good in this") that she became willing to take the wheel—literally.

Mary learned a lot from that experience. We all laugh about it now, mostly because it's one of the few times she's been able to be accused of any sort of laziness. But that's what this deadly does: it disguises itself as something else.

Is fear keeping you from being your best?

SLOTH

THE PHONE

I think my kids have always had better things to do than talk with me. Ben was 8 and Mary was 4. I called from work, looking for Dad. But Ben answered the phone. His first words were, "Hi, Mom," followed almost immediately by, "Here, you can talk to Mare."

He then passed the phone off to his sister, who said in a somewhat more interested voice, "Oh, Hi, Mommy." It had been almost 30 minutes since I had left the house, so I asked her how she was. "I'm really good," was her reply. I then asked if she could go get Daddy so I could talk with him. "Mmm, I don't think so. I don't feel like getting him. You can call back later. 'Kay, Bye, Mommy!"

Click.

Just wait until she's in college and she calls home for money.

I am so thankful that God doesn't tell us to call back later. He is right here, waiting for you. He wants you to simply come. He's ready to listen, ready to talk, ready to be worshipped.

He'll never hang up on you.

SLOTH

HEAVY

It was after Thanksgiving Dinner, and I was whipping some, er, whipping cream in a bowl. Curious, Mary, then fours year old, grabbed a stool, brought it over next to me, jumped up on it, and leaned on the counter as she asked, "Whatcha doin', Mommy?"

"I'm making whipping cream."

"How do you make it?"

I explained, "See that carton next to you? It looks like a milk carton, doesn't it? Inside is some really heavy milk. I pour the heavy milk in the bowl, and I mix it until it gets really fluffy." I didn't figure that she needed to know the rest of the recipe of sugar and vanilla.

Clearly, the issue of the cream was plenty to deal with, as I watched her focus her attention on the now mostly empty carton of whipping cream. Staring the carton down, she finally grabbed the carton with both hands. Ready to hoist the carton, she found she could lift it quite easily. Stunned, Mary turned to me and said, "Mommy, you're wrong. The milk isn't heavy. See? I can pick it up with only one hand!"

Trying to explain to a child something difficult, like the difference between whipping cream and milk, can be quite a challenge.

I wonder if that's how the disciples felt at that Last Supper, as Jesus broke the bread and told them that it was His body. I wonder if they gave Jesus the same "what in the *world* are you talking about" look as my daughter gave to me when I was trying to explain whipping cream.

It's pretty easy to dismiss things in our life that don't make sense. The sin of sloth slithers in when we discount what The Lord is saying to us because we're not fully tuned into Him. We explain away an awful lot of miracles because we don't understand what He's doing. It's easier to steer clear of spiritual disciplines, and to shy away from devoting time to building a relationship with the King of Kings, and to live by our own rules, than to have faith that someone greater than I already has this well in hand.

Easier, maybe. But never is it better.

This life goes by a lot faster than we realize. In fact, it's the blink of an eternal eye. We don't have to have it all figured out, but we do have the opportunity to live it well by trusting that God knows exactly what He's doing.

Is there something in your life that you are focusing hard on figuring out yourself--or controlling--or denying--and not letting The Lord know that you trust Him in even this?

Have a little faith.

It'll go a long way.

SLOTH

SO WHAT?

Look at these words from the writer of Hebrews:
Hebrews 6:10-12

> *[10]God is not unjust; he will not forget your work and the love you have shown him as you have helped his people and continue to help them. [11]We want each of you to show this same diligence to the very end, in order to make your hope sure. [12]We do not want you to become lazy, but to imitate those who through faith and patience inherit what has been promised.*

Sloth is a major theme in our world. We're a culture of the complacent, a community dedicated to leisure. For most of us, our diversions distract us more than they restore us.

We have an opportunity to be diligent in faith. The spiritual issues of our day are enormous, as we find ourselves "busy" with things that have no eternal worth. But Hebrews 6 gives us an alternative: diligence. It's a character trait that can become the focus of the Christian, rather than letting exhaustion from things that don't matter be what takes over.

Do you remember Matthew 11:28-30? It goes like this:

> *[28]"Come to me, all you who are weary and burdened, and I will give you rest. [29]Take my yoke upon you and learn from me, for I am gentle and humble in heart, and you will find rest for your souls. [30]For my yoke is easy and my burden is light."*

Matthew 11:28-30 gives us the offer of rest; this gift is the authentic goal the slothful are seeking in their broken way. What we seek in sloth is what we can only find in Christ: true rest, true peace, true life.

Maybe now is your chance to commit a portion of your day to the Lord, whether it's in reading a devotional, or studying Scripture, or getting on your knees and praying—really praying, not that *"Oh, did I fall asleep last night while I was repeating the same thing over and over again in my prayer? Oops"* prayer. See, we've all been there.

Perhaps you're at a point in your life where you can take a spiritual inventory. What are you spending your time on? Is it Kingdom work, or stuff you "have to do"? We are invited to give to the Lord of every part of our lives; your time is part of your gift. Your time can sometimes seem to be a hotter commodity—and in shorter supply—than even your money.

Maybe you're at a place in your life where it's time to consider "Retirement with a Purpose." Understand what it is you are retiring *for*...and what you are retiring *from*. You have an opportunity to share your wisdom and minister to young and old alike in ways your community has never seen. Teenagers are looking for direction, even when they act like they know everything, and you can be a loving presence in their lives. Adults are running around with their heads cut off; you have a chance to be Jesus to them. Teach a class, mentor a child, pray for a pastor.

Decide how you are going to serve Christ in a new way and not fall into the sin of sloth. If you can get up and around, then get up and around. Serve in another part of the world. Or stay in town. Don't let physical abilities or disabilities keep you from serving The Lord wherever you are. Write a note of encouragement. Pick up the phone and call someone who needs to hear a word of peace or assurance. Or, stay right where you are, fold your hands, bow your head, and pray for the person who comes to your mind.

Start reading the Bible. Keep reading the Bible. Turn off the television and turn on your faith.

Jesus is right next to you, right now. Don't tune Him out, today... or ever.

Too many people are depending on you. Give them Jesus, and then watch out.

You just might be amazed at the results God has in store for them. And you.

CONCLUSION

Pride Envy Gluttony Lust Anger Greed Sloth

The Race

My two friends had made a simple request: walk a half marathon with us.

C'mon. It'll be fun.

I made no preparations. After all, I've been putting one foot in front of the other for years, right? How tough can it be?

Until we got to Portland, Oregon, where we joined the twelve thousand or so others who had jumped into their single-digit-sized running gear and strapped on their perfectly packed gear belts and filled their ears with inspirational Rocky-style music coming from the latest technological wonder that was attached to the upper arm.

I had no fancy garb--just my old running pants (which looked just fine...and I had never used for running); my running shoes (that I had bought the day before--those things don't need to be broken in, do they?); no music--because I was walking with my friends and we'd have plenty to talk about; no fancy power bars or power gel or power gummy bears--I knew there were going to be tables of water along the way, so I figured all the extra stuff was just a ploy to get runners to buy more unnecessary garb.

I had none of it. And I was fine. *After all, we're just walking, right?*

Yeah, right...right up until the race started. That gun went off, and my two friends took off.

Running.

So I did the only thing I could do. I started running, too.

I made it almost to the one-mile marker before, huffing and puffing, I let them go. By the time I passed that one-mile mark, I started crying.

12.1 more miles to go.

I thought I was ready for this. But I hadn't prepared at all. I didn't have the tools, I hadn't gotten into shape, I hadn't focused--at all--on what this race would mean or how I was going to cross the finish line.

After the race, I found my friends at a local restaurant. They had been celebrating their finish for over an hour by the time I arrived on the scene. I was embarrassed that I hadn't trained. I was shocked that I couldn't have faked it and kept up with them. I was humiliated that I had let my body go to such an extent that even walking that far made me sore for a week afterward.

My experience with that half marathon was a life-changer. I got home, and (although my body was screaming to just chalk it all up to experience and move on) I decided I was going to try it again the next year, but this time I would do it differently. So, for the next 365 days, I trained for the race. I got out and ran nearly every day. On cold or rainy days, I hopped onto my 12-year-old treadmill and walked and ran with the race in mind.

Hebrews 12 was great inspiration for me as I took to the road each morning before anyone else got up:

> *...Let us run with perseverance the race marked out for us, fixing our eyes on Jesus, the pioneer and perfecter of faith. For the joy set before him he endured the cross, scorning its shame, and sat down at the right hand of the throne of God. Consider him who endured such opposition from sinners, so that you will not grow weary and lose heart.*

My goal was to run half of the race. And when the next year's half marathon came around, I ran more than 7 miles of the course (a personal best--I'd never run more than 4 miles at any one time during my training), and I shaved over an hour off my previous year's record.

I was so proud of my achievement. It was the fulfillment of a year-long dream. I envisioned the following year's race. I proudly displayed a "13.1" sticker on the back of my car.

And then, a week after the race, I started to hurt.

Something was wrong with my hip. I tried to keep running, but the pain was enough that running turned to walking, and then I skipped a day, and then another, then tried to get on the treadmill and kept tripping, and pretty soon, I had a hard time just getting into my car, as both hips had given out.

That's when my illustration of faith, of running with perseverance, of keeping my eyes on the prize, became all about me. *What if I gain the weight I've lost? What if I stop looking as good as my husband keeps saying I look these days? What if I turn into a sloth? What do I say when people ask me if I'm still running?*

I had turned this marathon into a high-profile experience. I thought it was a great example of what The Lord can do, but I realized that it didn't take much to make it all about me. I marinated in self-pity as I watched my body lose a lot of its tone. I became frustrated and aggravated as I struggled to make it up the two steps of our walk into our home. I glared with envy at runners along the street that I would drive by every day when I was out in my car. One surgery became two, and two became four. I now have hips that light up the scanners at the airport. I had to give up running, but I am able to start each morning on the elliptical machine. I no longer play tennis (which was my first love), but my husband and now I walk all over town.

My running story is no tragedy. Most of the time I remember to be giving thanks to The Lord that I'm even able to be upright. When I don't feel like getting up at oh-early-thirty to get on the elliptical, I usually remind myself of that year of not being able to exercise, which is--usually--all it takes.

It's pretty easy to turn a gift from The Lord into an accomplishment of mine. I did the work, I get the prize. But His prize is ever so much greater than any medallion I'll receive for crossing the finish line of a marathon.

This story is an example of pride: Look at me and how strong I am. It is an example of envy: When I was unable to run, I wanted what those other runners had, and I seethed inside because they had it and I didn't. It's about gluttony, because never was I satisfied. It's about lust: When I was down, I thought, *Right now, I should be the one running, and I want all the fancy equipment that is sure to make me a great athlete.* It was about anger when I couldn't get what I wanted, it was about greed (just a little bit more--more speed, more praise, more winner shirts, more donations, another pair of running shoes). And it was about sloth, because I came to focus on the running for my sake, and not focus on ways I could reach out for the Lord. I was so busy feeling sorry for myself that I became lazy about what the Lord might be teaching me in that time. You name it, I wanted it...in order to be a better athlete that is focused on The Lord, of course. Of course.

I can think of a thousand stories to exemplify these sins. Perhaps you could think of a few from your life as well...if you try really, really hard.

Or, you could turn your stories into examples of when you were humble, and complimentary, and a good steward, and gracious, and happy, and content, and on-fire for The Lord. And, when you do, share them.

People want to hear.